The Revd Canon Dr Alan Billings is an Anglican priest and a former Director of the Centre for Ethics and Religion at Lancaster University. He previously trained clergy in a number of institutions: he was Vice Principal of Ripon College, Cuddesdon; Principal of the West Midlands Ministerial Training Course and acting Principal of Queens College, Birmingham; and taught pastoral studies at the College of the Resurrection, Mirfield. He has been Deputy Leader of Sheffield City Council, a member of the Archbishop's Commission on Urban Priority Areas (*Faith in the City*), and a member of the Home Office Community Cohesion Panel following the riots of 2001. He contributes regularly to BBC Radio 4's 'Thought for the day' and is a board member of the Youth Justice Board for England and Wales and the Big Lottery Fund, England Committee. His other books for SPCK are *Making God Possible* (2010); *God and Community Cohesion* (2009); *Secular Lives Sacred Hearts* (2004) and *Dying and Grieving* (2002).

T0316296

LOST CHURCH

Why we must find it again

Alan Billings

First published in Great Britain in 2013

Society for Promoting Christian Knowledge
36 Causton Street
London SW1P 4ST
www.spckpublishing.co.uk

British Library Cataloguing-in-Publication Data
A catalogue record for this book is available from the British Library

ISBN 978–0–281–07019–0
eBook ISBN 978–0–281–07020–6

Typeset by Graphicraft Limited, Hong Kong
First printed in Great Britain by Ashford Colour Press
Subsequently digitally printed in Great Britain

Produced on paper from sustainable forests

For Celeste and Eleanor

Contents

Acknowledgements

This book came out of conversations with many people. While none of them should be held responsible for anything that I have written, I would like to acknowledge how speaking with them and listening to them stimulated and clarified my own thinking. In particular I thank people I have met, clerical and lay, at Sheffield Cathedral, St Mary's Parish Church, Walkley, Sheffield, at the Urban Theology Unit, Sheffield, and on the Yorkshire Ministry Course, Mirfield and York.

In particular I thank at St Mary's: The Revd Melanie FitzGerald, The Revd Shan Rush, The Revd Sarah Walsh, Carol Hawke, Barbara Waterhouse, Vicky Romegoux, Lynne Ross, Kath Boyd, Anne and Peter Grant, Catherine Burchell, Siobhan and Howard Hoyes, Janet Elsden, Judith Keeton, Joyce Gambling, Helen, Geoff and Matthew Vause, Shirley Moore, David Clark, Joe Pritchard, Lynette Jackson, Mary Rushby, Lynne Warren, Lynne Simpson, Violet Ashton, Judith Gilmour, John Furness, Irving Smith, Hope Everson, Dennis Gratton, Helen and Elijah Boyle, Julie Mason, Steve Grimshaw, Sally Terris, Jo and Paul Russell, and the late Bill Gibb. They have taught me a great deal concerning what a Church of England congregation is all about.

I owe thanks too for the preaching of the Dean of Sheffield, The Very Revd Peter Bradley, and the cathedral clergy – Canons Simon Cowling, Chris Burke and Dr Joanne Grenfell. Also to the cathedral congregation, especially Ken and Sarah Bowler and Michael Jarratt.

At the Urban Theology Unit I owe particular thanks to The Revd Dr John Vincent and The Revd Dr Ian Duffield. On the Yorkshire Ministry Course I thank The Revd Tim Evans and the students.

Acknowledgements

I am grateful to my wife, Veronica, for allowing me to spend time with the word processor. Alison Barr, at SPCK, has been, as ever, encouraging and helpful at all times.

Alan Billings
Sheffield

Introduction

It is hard to navigate this post-religious relativist age.

Janice Turner, The Times columnist and non-believer

In 1994, Grace Davie, a sociologist of religion, wrote a book about religion in Britain since 1945. In it she sought to explain the relationship between the British people and the Christian faith. She captured one of her principal findings in the book's subtitle: *Believing without belonging.*[1] The British might not be great church attenders – which is what Davie meant by 'belonging' – but they did believe in God and they were content to call themselves Christians. The idea has been very influential. For many clergy, faced with declining congregations, it offered some cheer, especially when they began to suffer the slings and arrows of a growing constituency of vocal and aggressive opponents of religion from the 1990s. They told themselves that the strength of religious faith in the country could not be captured by statistics of church attendance or organized religious observance alone; account must also be taken of how people answered questions about religious belief that opinion pollsters put to them. In survey after survey, a majority affirmed their belief in God. This was subsequently reflected in the 2001 Census, in which 72 per cent of the population claimed a Christian identity.[2] Professor Davie seemed vindicated: there was believing without belonging (attending). The clergy were encouraged. The glass was half full!

As a parish priest at the time, I was never wholly persuaded that the British were 'believing without belonging', and I am even less convinced now. It did not seem to reflect the reality of what clergy encounter week by week in their local communities.

More than that, it led us all the time to make other binary distinctions that blinded us to the true situation. We thought that people were either 'believers' or 'unbelievers', 'attenders' or 'non-attenders'. I want to suggest that this way of thinking has been seriously misleading. In particular, it overlooks the most significant category of all: those who – in a sense I will explain – 'belong' but who do not attend regularly or believe coherently or consistently, or at all. These people – those who belong – are the majority. Yet since we have not understood the nature of this 'belonging' or who these people are, we have often failed in our mission and ministry towards them, the majority of our neighbours. What I attempt to do in this book, therefore, is highlight this other category: as well as those who 'attend' and those who 'believe', and those who neither attend nor believe, there are also those who 'belong' – who may or may not believe and who only attend on certain occasions! If the British are anything, they are those who 'belong'.

There was a time when the Church of England instinctively knew who the 'belongers' were and accepted that it had responsibilities towards them. This is why it has retained the geographical organization of the Church. The Church of England is parish-based – or it ceases to be the Church of England. This was the assumption informing all the liturgies of the Book of Common Prayer. This was how clergy historically thought of their role in society: all the people of England 'belonged' – unless they exempted themselves – and the Church had a responsibility towards every community. In turn, this was the compact that the 'belongers' also understood and accepted. While they might struggle with beliefs and not wish to attend church regularly, they did, in some misty way, feel the Church had some legitimate part to play in their lives and could be called upon when needed. On the whole, despite the advance of secularism and a growing pluralism in both organized religion and personal faith, most people have not stopped thinking in these terms; but the Church has. This is the Church we have lost. This book, therefore, is an attempt to recall Anglicans, lay and ordained, to their historic mission by reminding them of that lost Church and why it must be found again for the sake of the general well-being of communities.

Is this the time?

In one respect this is not an easy time to make this case. Those who argue as I do are vigorously assailed from two directions. On the one hand, there are some very vocal Anglicans who have completely given up on the traditional form of the Church of England and advocate instead a different model of the Church. In part this is an argument from practicality – resources are becoming scarcer and maintaining the parish system spreads them too thinly. In part it is a theological argument – an insistence that a Christian congregation should only consist of committed believers. On the other hand, there are strident atheists who have no time for the Church or Christianity in any shape at all. I will say more about the Christian critics in the following pages and particularly in the final chapter, but I would note here that as far as British atheism goes, I do believe we are beginning to see some change in attitudes. The stridency and sheer aggression of past years and the total rejection of religion seem to have passed their high-water mark. There are signs that a tide is turning, and some of those who have been more noted for their criticism of Christianity in the past have taken a second look at the role religion and the Church plays in the lives of individuals and communities and have begun to be more nuanced in their comments and even appreciative of what faith does. I will expand on this in later chapters, but one straw in the wind will make the point for the moment. The naturalist and broadcaster Sir David Attenborough, well known as a non-believer, told listeners to BBC Radio 4's *Desert Island Discs* in January 2012 that while he remains 'agnostic' he does not believe that evolution is incompatible with belief in God and he was 'not so confident as to say that I'm an atheist'. Attenborough has not been the only non-believer who has been taking a more conciliatory approach recently – as I shall show.

What I argue throughout the book is that the place of religion in British society and the lives of individuals is far more complex than we once thought. Far from turning its back on faith, contemporary Britain presents quite different challenges in which the traditional parish church continues to have a role. But we need to appreciate and understand just what is happening.

The book in outline

I begin the book by rejecting the binary distinction that Professor Davie made between those who believe and those who belong. Instead, I propose three categories and seek to distinguish between them:

- those who belong
- those who believe
- those who attend.

The categories are not necessarily mutually exclusive. Some will find themselves in all three, some in two, some in one. (Many, of course, are in none.) I examine each of these in separate chapters. I also seek to show that for an understanding of the continuing role of the Church of England, the most important of these groups of people are those who feel they 'belong'. In the final chapter I attempt to say why I think Professor Davie's distinction has misled a generation of clergy by encouraging them to concentrate on one aspect of the Church's mission – evangelism – to the neglect of others. This has produced a dissatisfaction with the traditional role of the Church of England and a gradual adoption of other ways of thinking about it.

The Church we have lost is the Church that understood the importance of those who belong but who might or might not believe, and who attend only as particular circumstances demand. It is this lost Church that I want Anglicans to find again. I begin, therefore, by explaining as carefully as I can who I think this majority is that still feels it belongs to the Church and the Christian faith, those for whom the Church of England has in the past felt a particular responsibility and who in turn still continue to have an affection for the Church.

1

Belonging

Just as there are many Jews who keep the Friday ritual in their home despite describing themselves as atheists, I am a 'tribal Christian', happy to attend church services.

Lord Rees, Master of Trinity College, Cambridge, and Astronomer Royal

In Britain an increasingly faithless land finds itself ironically turning to faith institutions as symbols of local cohesion. Long may such places survive.

Simon Jenkins, The Guardian *columnist and non-believer*

I suggested in the Introduction that we need to understand the relationship of the British to Christianity and the Church according to three categories: belonging, believing and attending. In this first chapter I will seek to explain and expand on what I mean by 'belonging'. I will differentiate it from attending and believing – though there will be some overlapping – and say why the idea of belonging is both important to understand and why it can be so easily misunderstood or overlooked. I will also suggest that a large part of the Christian constituency in this country consists of those who belong. They are in addition to those who attend. In both of these groups – belongers and attenders – there will be believers; though some may belong or attend and not believe. If this sounds complex it is because the religious situation is more complex than the usual binary divisions – believer/non-believer, attender/non-attender – suggest. But if the Churches lose sight of those who belong they will not understand how the nation may still be considered Christian.

If the Church of England loses sight of them, it will cease to be the national Church whatever its constitutional position. It will have disestablished itself.

Those who 'belong' to Christianity and the Church are not an entirely homogeneous group; but there are some things we can say about them. In the first place, most of them, though not all, would define themselves as Christians even though they rarely attend church. They struggle to articulate any beliefs, because for them Christianity is not primarily a matter of beliefs. Some are not believers in any orthodox sense, and some are not believers at all. This latter group may be the most puzzling of all. We are used to the idea of the secular Jew, but not the secular Christian.

In what sense, then, are those who do call themselves Christians but do not attend church Christian? They are Christian because in terms of the Christian faith they respond positively to the life, teaching and example of Jesus Christ. They seek to base their own lives as best they may on what they believe he stood for and taught: they want to be as generous, merciful, forgiving and loving as he was. They are also positive in their attitude towards the Church. They are not hostile to its ministers, whom they believe do valuable work in the community, not least when individuals or communities are struggling or in need. They do not regard church buildings as alien places or church services as alien activities. But they see no reason to attend regularly and they have little time for creeds, confessions of faith or theology. There is a smaller group who would call themselves 'non-believers' yet still think Christianity has value and believe society is better for having churches; they do not want the Christian Church to disappear from the land. There can be many variations on these themes, but taken together, those who in some sense 'belong' to Christianity and the Church are a very large part of the general population. They are probably most people.

But those who 'belong' are generally unrecognized and uncounted: they will not show up in the Census data as a discrete category or an identifiable group and opinion pollsters would have difficulty framing a question that would enable us to identify them. Yet it is especially important for the Church of England as the national Church to understand what belonging is and who the 'belongers' are. If the Church is to remain credible and to have any social value beyond its own regular congregations, it needs to acknowledge that many people continue to have a sense of belonging. If it can do that, it will continue to find ways in which it can serve that wider constituency. If it fails to do so, it will condemn itself to eventual social irrelevancy. But time is short and the omens are not all good.

Walking away from organized religion

In saying that the British 'belong', I am not denying for one moment the truth of the statistical evidence that Grace Davie amassed in her 1994 book, and which has continued to be gathered since. This shows that the British people have stopped attending churches in any numbers. They have been walking away from organized religion throughout the later twentieth century. There is little point in revisiting all of that data since it is now well known and broadly accepted. Whatever statistics we choose to consider – from numbers on electoral rolls to communicant or baptism figures – and while there might have been an increase in Christian practice in the first ten years or so after the Second World War, the decline from the end of the 1950s is undeniable and continuing. We need to recognize the gravity of that situation and the amount of ground that has been lost: as far as attending goes, in Britain in the early decades of the twenty-first century, churchgoing is reaching an all-time and critical low point. In addition, religion is no longer something taken in with mother's milk. Each new generation knows less about the content of the faith and becomes less 'attuned' to religious experience. This is reflected in the fact that in answers to opinion pollsters and in the latest National Census, more people than ever are prepared to say they have 'no religious beliefs'. According to the 2009 British Social Attitudes Survey, those who profess no religious belief have been steadily rising – from 31 per cent in 1983 to 51 per cent in 2009.[1] Religion no longer plays a conscious role in the lives of most people – though that is not the same as saying it plays no unconscious role or no role at all. But for at least a substantial number of people, the truths to which the Church has historically borne witness are no longer taken for granted.

As the Church began to be uncomfortably aware of the extent of this change and to the fall in regular attenders, it turned its attention to the need to halt and reverse the decline. But here it made a fatal mistake. It failed to distinguish between believing, attending and belonging – and conflated the last two. As a result, those whom I have called 'belongers' disappeared from sight: there could only be attenders/non-attenders and believers/non-believers – the binary divisions that I have said offer an inadequate analysis.

So who are those who 'belong' but do not attend and do not necessarily have much if anything by way of belief? How are we to recognize them? How numerous are they and how are we to support them?

The persistence of 'belonging'

Between 2000 and 2002, researchers from Lancaster University conducted a survey of the religious commitments and sensibilities of people in the town of Kendal in Cumbria, where I was a parish priest. They found all the indices of church decline that I mentioned above and the rise of alternative, 'holistic' spiritualities as well. In addition, when some of the researchers went from door to door and interviewed residents in selected streets, they made another important discovery.[2] This was that most people were neither religious nor anti-religious but, most of the time, simply indifferent.[3] This 'most of the time' is an important qualification, as we shall see. Most of the time, they could see few reasons for becoming involved in a church or thinking too much or too often about Christian beliefs. What could either bring to their lives? As a result, they never had reason to discuss religious matters with their spouses or partners whose religious sensibilities, if they had any, were completely unknown to them. The researchers found that while some women might discuss some aspect of religion with their women friends – on a girls' night out, for instance – men never would. They simply could not see how religion might add value to the way they lived. Most parish priests who have any serious engagement with people beyond their congregations will recognize what I describe as part of contemporary reality.

In light of this general indifference, we learn two important lessons. The first is that indifference is not the same as hostile rejection. The British people have been influenced by two decades of attack on belief by the New Atheists, but it has left many, perhaps the majority, indifferent rather than convinced unbelievers. They are certainly no more impressed by strident atheism than they are by strident Christianity. But they are open to persuasion – if they can see the value of religion to human life, something that enables them to live well because it sustains the values they think important.

The second lesson is that this indifference was 'most of the time' and not 'all of the time'. There could be occasions when the Church might have something to say or to offer. Indeed, on these occasions, the Church might be the only institution to which people could turn. We need, therefore, to be very attentive to those times when the ministry of the Church is sought and to think carefully about what they tell us. In a more secular age, this is a matter of greater significance than it was in a time when religion was taken for granted. It means that people who, for instance, seek a christening for their child are going against the secular grain of contemporary society. That is a more significant act than asking for baptism in a time when the majority of children were baptized. Such parents may well have to explain their behaviour to family or friends and be a little clearer in their own mind why they are doing it. Equally, the Church needs to understand that it is able to offer something of value unavailable elsewhere.

When 'belonging' shows itself

The fact is that the ministry of the Church is still sought by people in certain circumstances. These circumstances may not occur every week, but they have not disappeared entirely. It is in this sense that I believe we need to speak of people who 'belong'. What we mean is that many people continue to feel some affinity with the Church (of England) and the faith it stands for and proclaims; they still feel able to ask for ministry in some form and on specific occasions; the local clergy are deemed approachable and on their side. Above all, we mean that there is a sizeable body of people who may not attend and who may not believe in any orthodox sense, or whose beliefs are not formulated as doctrines or who do not believe at all, but who still feel that there are occasions on which the Church can supply meaning or be pastorally helpful.

Anglicans should not be surprised by this since we have encouraged people to feel this way for the whole of our history. Indeed, this takes us to the heart of what the Church of England is about.[4] We have taught people down the five centuries of our existence that everyone lives in a parish, and everyone in that parish is welcome at the parish church. We expect people to hold a range of theological views; we are a broad Church; we have no pope or curia. The 'vicar' is not just the ecclesiastical leader of one Christian church among many, but 'our vicar'; everyone can lay claim to him or her and can call on their services. In these ways, the Church of England has encouraged the development of this idea of 'belonging'. This is something 'tribal' – though not in the sense that it seeks to exclude. On the contrary, this is a tribe that welcomes all people who inhabit a particular place – the parishes of England. Lord Rees, the Astronomer Royal, summed up one important aspect of this when he said that he was happy to attend Anglican services even though he was not a believer, and hoped to be buried in a country churchyard according to the rites of the Anglican Church; these were the rituals of his tribe. He belongs.[5]

'Belonging', in the sense I am defining it, makes itself apparent at different times and in many different situations. But it can easily be misunderstood. The Church that recognizes what it is to belong, and believes that this is something to be welcomed, encouraged and sustained, is the Church we have almost lost and need to recover.

Let me give some examples of how the sense of belonging continues to show itself and how it may be lost. I will comment on a range of different situations before finally seeking to summarize what all of these instances have in common.

Times of community solidarity

We can probably all agree that one feature of contemporary society is the loss, or at any rate the weakening, of any sense of community. The attempt by the Prime Minister and the Conservative–Liberal Democrat government after 2010 to bring to birth the 'Big Society' was a response to that. There was a feeling that while society had become more prosperous, and that was a great gain, modern city living in particular had made us more individualistic and less inclined to join with others in any community activity. This was resulting in greater social separation than in the past, and this showed itself in more people becoming isolated in later life, especially as they tended to live longer. As we go through life, our chances for making new friends often diminish. Once we retire from work we are increasingly thrown back on a few old friends and our families. If they move away or fail us we can be left lonely and on our own. Moreover, in an age of austerity the state is not able to step in and help as it might once have done. Hence the need for a revival of community life, the Big Society.

There are times when a local community or the nation as a whole needs to come together. These may be times of celebration, commemoration, perplexity or mourning. In the past, people would have turned quite naturally and easily to the Churches and would have taken part in religious services where appropriate emotions were articulated and interpreted in the light of the Christian faith, and where people who might otherwise be relative strangers to one another were enabled to meet. But in a more plural society this becomes more difficult to handle – difficult but not impossible. What the Churches, especially the Church of England, have learnt to do over the years is to make such occasions as inclusive as possible. This has happened best when the clergy have understood that there exists this category of people who may be infrequent attenders and hesitant believers but who nevertheless 'belong'. Trust can be built between Church and 'belongers' in the wider community that enables clergy to exercise leadership and to minister at those moments when the community or the nation needs to come together for some specific reason.

At a national level, St Paul's Cathedral and Westminster Abbey are skilled at enabling diverse groups of people to join together on many different kinds of occasion: to give thanks for the end of a war; to rejoice at the marriage of a royal prince; to commemorate a great writer or poet; to mourn a statesman or monarch. In local communities, the clergy stand ready to help manage complex emotions when some tragedy happens. When, for example, the people of Soham in Cambridgeshire were shocked to discover that two of their children had been murdered by the caretaker of their school, they were able to look to the churches for help because the clergy – in this case Methodist and Anglican – instinctively understood that they could help those in the wider community because the wider community accepted that this was an appropriate role for them to play. The parish church opened its doors and enabled people in shock and grief to light candles, lay flowers, sit quietly or say prayers. They arranged services in which appropriate words could be said and hymns sung – how we value the traditional hymn book with its rich theology and diverse themes on these occasions! In the same way, when a lone gunman, Derrick Bird, began shooting and killing people in Whitehaven, Cumbria, in 2010, the focus for the community's emotion – its grief and sadness, its perplexity and, yes, its anger too – were the churches. The rituals and words that brought comfort to many were mainly those of Christianity – the lighting of candles in churches, the laying of flowers in the graveyards, the funerals and memorial services. The people entrusted with enabling this to take place appropriately and with sensitivity were the clergy of the local churches. The clergy were able to speak for many because their role at such a time was accepted. They already had the trust of the community to be able to act on their behalf. This ministry is only possible where both Church and people implicitly recognize the category of 'those who belong' but who are not necessarily committed attenders or believers.

But this can be lost. It takes great skill on the part of the clergy to manage these occasions. If they fail to articulate well the thoughts and feelings of those in perplexity or distress, or fail to acknowledge that those present may not all share the same beliefs, or try to turn these occasions into opportunities for explicit evangelism, the compact between Church and 'belongers' will be damaged. Not all contemporary Anglican clergy are willing to play this role. Not all Anglican clergy in training have received any help in thinking about it.

Pastoral services

The sense of belonging also shows itself on those occasions when the pastoral offices of the Church are directly sought.

Although there has been a decline in the number of marriages, baptisms and funerals, many continue to ask for them. But this 'asking' is, in contemporary culture, quite different from asking in more traditional society. In societies where religious belief was taken for granted, people turned to the Church when they married, had a child or when their loved ones died, because that is what every member of society did. These events of the life cycle – giving birth, marriage and death – were understood in the light of Christian faith. The Church gave them their meaning and there were few, if any, rival accounts. But now, asking for one of the pastoral services runs counter to the secular temper. This means for some of those who come seeking one or other of the pastoral offices that they have to explain themselves to others in a way that would have been inconceivable before the later decades of the last century. It requires a more decisive act than in the past. It may be quite courageous. In such circumstances, people are only able to ask for ministry if they feel they have some proper claim on the Church and its ministers: if they feel they, in some sense, belong. This is in part a legacy of the traditional society of the past. But if that were all, it would gradually disappear as society became more distanced from that past age. But the sense of belonging can be more than that: it can be a deeply rooted sentiment that can be encouraged and sustained if the Church and its clergy continue to welcome people at those significant moments in their lives. Equally, of course, it can be lost if the Church and its clergy are perceived as placing obstacles in the way or making unreasonable demands, or if they simply refuse to continue to offer this ministry. If we look at each of the pastoral offices, we find that this is precisely what was happening for much of the last forty or so years.

Infant baptism

There is no doubt that the Church has made it more difficult for people to have their children baptized, sometimes deliberately, sometimes unintentionally. Long before the Reformation, baptism had become a rite associated with giving birth and having children, rather than with the initiation of adults into the Christian faith. The Church of England accepted the view of the majority of the Reformers, such as Martin Luther and John Calvin, and continued to baptize infants; and this was the settled practice for the next four hundred years. However, after the Second World War there was a general unease about infant baptism and a lively debate ensued. There was agreement across the theological/ecclesiastical spectrum that children should not be baptized in the way the Book of Common Prayer envisaged. One of the rubrics at the head of the service of 'The Ministration of Publick Baptism of Infants' reads:

> When there are children to be baptized, the Parents shall give knowledge thereof over night, or in the morning before the beginning of Morning Prayer.

The clergy have increasingly turned away from this Prayer Book approach. It could not possibly be encouraged in a time when, it was assumed, people sat rather more lightly to Christian faith. It suggested a degree of casualness that the modern Church, anxious about belief and attendance, could not countenance. Accordingly, while many clergy insisted on parents coming to preparation classes or courses, others offered alternatives to baptism – dedication or thanksgiving. There were also those – ordained despite holding an understanding of baptism that was alien to the Prayer Book – who refused to baptize children at all. Some Anglican churches have even 're-baptized' those who were baptized as infants. (Astonishingly, the Archbishop of York baptized a woman who had been baptized in infancy at an open-air baptism outside the Minster in 2012.[6]) Many made little or no effort to try to understand what motivates parents and what baptism might mean to them. Parents asked for bread and were frequently offered a stone.

Since we have often not understood the way in which people 'belong', we have not always been able to understand what parents say about the baptism of their children. We are so anxious to impart our own meanings to baptism that we have not always been willing to hear the meanings the parents already attach to it themselves – which is why they seek it. If we take the time to listen we may be humbled and astonished at what we hear. For instance, I once asked a young mother why she did not want a thanksgiving service for the birth of her child, but a baptism. She was more articulate than many and explained that what made the crucial difference was the water rite. Slowly and carefully she said this – which I wrote down immediately afterwards! I have taken it as my guide for what mothers want ever since:

> When you hold the baby at the christening it's like me holding him at bath-time. I wash him clean and make him really beautiful before he goes to bed. It's a wonderful time. In some ways it's the best time of the day. He's clean and smells fresh and lovely – and I love him as if for the first time all over again. When you wash him you make him spiritually fragrant and I think God loves him then in the same way.[7]

'Spiritually fragrant' – her words made me gasp when she spoke them. I had not thought that this is what I was doing, at a baptism, but I have never been able to get the words out of my head since that evening. In all subsequent baptisms I have held the child even more carefully and deliberately, as if I were washing him or her at bath-time. 'When you wash him you make him spiritually fragrant' – that seemed to be as good a way of explaining being 'regenerate and born anew of Water and of the Holy Ghost' as anyone could require of someone who was not a professional theologian.

A bishop once told me that he sympathized with those clergy who refused baptism to parents who 'clearly did not believe anything'. What a strange thing to say. Parents may be inarticulate, especially when faced by clergy who have the power to say 'yes' or 'no' to their request for baptism. They do not want to say the 'wrong' thing, so they say little or nothing; but no one brings their child to church, hands him or her over to a stranger and invites them to pour water over them, without thinking something and believing something. Parents, especially mothers, can sometimes think about the baptism of their children in the most profound ways, as I have shown. But we are often so busy explaining our point of view that we fail to make time for or frame the conditions in which parents might give voice to their own understanding. In a more secular culture, parents are at least as likely to have thought about what baptism means for them as in a more religious age, and perhaps more likely, even though they will do this in non-theological language. If a degree of trust can be built with the priest, they will slowly articulate their thoughts.

People will go on asking for baptism for their children only if they continue to feel genuinely welcome in church. In recent years that has been placed in doubt. Infant baptism has been refused to many, or only made possible after the completion of some obstacle course, and this has distanced large numbers of people from the Church. The freemasonry of mothers in every parish has soon spread the word that this or that church or priest does not make welcome people seeking baptism. The sense of belonging is thereby eroded or lost. The same is true of the other pastoral services.

Marriage

Marriages in the Church of England have now fallen to about 24 per cent of all marriages – and marriage itself has dropped out of favour. Although the Church has made a real attempt more recently to help couples marry in church – there is, for instance, a very good website – it has not always made it easy for those who feel they belong to the Church of England to get married there.[8] In particular, the Church was slow to respond to the consequences of greater mobility, increased prosperity, higher divorce rates and changes in general social attitudes.

The population became more mobile and many young people found themselves living away from the parishes in which they had grown up and where their parents continued to live. Yet the Church at first insisted that they marry in the parish where they were then living and not in the places associated with their family histories. With growing prosperity, more and more couples sought to hold their receptions in hotels and other attractive venues, often many miles from their homes. Many would have liked a religious wedding in the building where the reception was being held; but the Church refused to countenance any change in the law to make this possible. The hotels and other venues were quick to respond, and the law was changed to allow them to hold a civil ceremony on their premises. Despite this, some couples still hoped that the clergy would at least be allowed to say prayers and bless their marriage at a hotel following a civil wedding – but again the Church disapproved. As a priest in the Lake District for more than a decade, I gloomily watched these developments and the lost opportunities they represented. One reason for the refusal to be flexible was a worthy attempt to protect the fee income of some of the less attractive parish churches, especially the Victorian and Edwardian churches of the inner city. This could only have worked had people wanted a church wedding more than they wanted a wedding in a convenient or aesthetically more appealing venue. It took the Church a long time to admit to itself what was happening.

All of this is surprising because there has never been any suggestion in Christian theology that for a marriage to be valid it had to be either conducted in a church or according to a particular ritual. Christianity did not invent marriage and Christ himself blessed with his presence and first miracle a village wedding at Cana-in-Galilee. Moreover, across the world and throughout human history, men and women have been marrying according to a great variety of practices and rituals. In many parts of continental Europe couples are married in a town hall or register office and then go to the church for a blessing. In other words, the Church can take a whole variety of marriage customs and traditions in its stride if it wants to. There is no theological reason why the Church of England should not have asked government to legislate to allow for a religious ceremony in a non-religious venue.

For many years divorce proved an insurmountable obstacle for many who wanted to marry in church. Although the rules here have been relaxed, it was not before very many people, including many regular attenders, were turned away because one or other partner had been divorced. For a time the Church made matters worse by allowing the re-marriage of some divorcees but not others and requiring the clergy to probe into people's past histories. The position ought to have been quite straightforward: if a couple were able to marry according to law, they should not have been prevented from marrying in church. By taking a different stance, the Church set itself up as an alternative to the civil courts. If the Church wanted to uphold the principle of marriage for life, this was at the price of seeming to be lacking in charity and denying people the possibility of making a new beginning – which, to many, seemed a more serious departure from the gospel. People were also not slow to notice that the Church began to relax its rules about re-marriage once clergy began to petition for divorce in significant numbers.

These are official decisions taken by the Church as a corporate body. We also have to add to them the eccentricities of individual clergy – for which there can be no legislation. In recent years, for example, some clergy seem to have taken against the singing of certain hymns at weddings: 'Jerusalem', 'All things bright and beautiful' and the Battle Hymn of the Republic have all featured in the media.

We are now faced with new possibilities: the blessing of civil partnerships, the blessing of homosexual couples in church

15

after a civil partnership, the marriage of gay couples. There seems little likelihood that the Church will allow any of these in the near future. Once again, the Church will be out of step with general opinion – at least on civil partnerships – and will struggle to explain itself. Most people outside the Church, and many if not most within, see this as a failure to affirm loving and faithful relationships in the light of contemporary under-standings of sexuality. They are not impressed by mainly Old Testament texts; they are impressed by the fact that Jesus does not seem to have directly commented on same-sex relationships; they suspect they know what his attitude would be if he were to comment now: 'It was said to you of old time, but I say unto you . . .'

We should note here an important difference between the Church of England and the Roman Catholic Church. Roman Catholics have an understanding of human sexuality and the purposes of marriage that make it very difficult for them to accept gay sexual relationships. Their position is derived from a mix of biblical texts and natural-law teaching. Central to this is the insistence that the purpose of sex is procreation and that the place for sexual activity is within marriage. Each sexual act must be open to at least the possibility of a child being conceived, and nothing must be done to frustrate this artificially. But the Church of England rejected such an approach in the last century when it allowed the possibility of contracep-tion and made it very clear in its revisions of the marriage service that marriage served purposes other than procreation. The mind of Anglicans has begun to move on the matter of gay relationships as well, though senior clergy probably lag behind lay Anglican opinion. In the meantime, lay people have had to furnish their own theological understanding of gay relations.

The damage done by the Church's refusal to accommodate people in these different situations extends beyond the offence given to the couple, their friends and family. Everyone else in society takes note. How, they wonder, is this consistent with the Church's witness to a God of love? What does it say about the Church's understanding of sexuality? How can the Church speak about human rights when it seems to be denying the fundamental right of two people of the same sex to have their union recognized? How does any of this support and uphold stable relationships?

Allowing civil partnerships or same-sex weddings in church is not a capitulation to the Zeitgeist; it is an acknowledgement that the Zeitgeist is ahead of the Church in realizing the moral implications of changes in how human sexuality is to be understood. In the meantime, many of those who instinctively feel they belong to the Church and Christianity are thoroughly disillusioned when they, members of their family or friends, are denied the ministry they seek. The sense of belonging erodes further.

Funerals

The Church has been more successful with funerals. It has learnt to respond to the requests of the bereaved when planning a funeral or memorial service, whether they are attenders or not, probably because parish clergy have been relatively free to make their own local decisions.

Clergy have learnt to 'personalize' the service by invoking the personality of the deceased – through the choice of readings and music, and in the address.[9] We have learnt to accept that Canon Henry Scott Holland's curious sentences that dismiss death as 'nothing at all' and dying as going into another room nearby will bring as much comfort as 'I am the resurrection and the life', while Frank Sinatra singing 'I did it my way' is as likely to greet us on the way into the crematorium as the playing of 'Sheep may safely graze'.

One of the biggest changes in funerals since the Second World War has been the gradual transformation of the sermon. Although the Book of Common Prayer saw no need to supplement the funeral liturgy with a sermon, post-war services have generally included one. In practice, sermons have gradually changed from being an attempt to explain the doctrine of the resurrection to being almost exclusively a tribute to the deceased. Clergy have also generally allowed the delivery of tributes by friends and relatives with minimal attempt to exercise any control over the material. (The address of Lord Spencer at the funeral of Princess Diana is only a high-profile instance of what has happened generally – and the risks involved.) But it has meant that mourners can be helped by hearing about their relative or friend 'in the round'.

More difficult to handle well is the fact that society is becoming ever more plural, so that the spectrum of possible beliefs that people may hold about death and its meaning is bewildering – and sometimes the chief mourner wants that acknowledged. On the whole, clergy have learnt that if they still want to minister to people through a funeral service they have to take a very tolerant view and prepare the congregation appropriately and early in the service. So, for example, the priest may begin by saying that on an occasion such as a funeral, people are present who understand the meaning of life and death in many different ways. A time of silence will be kept so that each person present can think their own thoughts. The priest may have to explain that while the deceased was well known in the community as a non-believer, his widow is a devout Christian, and the Christian funeral will help her in her grieving, something that her always charitable partner would well understand. Or the priest might explain that the readings and music will reflect the fact that the couple were from Christian and Buddhist traditions, while many of their friends were non-believers; and there will be an opportunity at the end of the service when 'each of us in our own way can remember the deceased and, if that is our custom, commend them to God'.

This is not hypocrisy. It is recognition that contemporary society is highly plural, and on this occasion the Church stands ready to help people express something of their differences in a way that enables all to feel included in saying an appropriate farewell. Contemporary congregations of diverse people are quite able to take account of any number of different approaches and traditions that might be expressed – as long as each is done sincerely, with integrity and due care for others. Each person's contribution is respected even if what is said does not reflect the views of everyone present. The pastoral task of the clergy – and this is a considerable skill – is to understand what is being requested and to convey to the congregation that what is said and done is said and done with the approval of the chief mourner or sometimes the deceased; and to hold all of that together within the framework afforded by the Christian liturgy. This in itself is a witness to the compassionate Lord.

Having a formal liturgy also performs other psychological and therapeutic tasks that are far more difficult to enable otherwise. A careful choice of readings, both scriptural and secular, and the use of particular prayers allow the expression of strong emotions of grief and mourning – sorrow, shock, loss, anger. Where someone has lived a less than saintly life, or where families have been fractured through quarrels or divorce, the possibility of some healing is offered through a judicious use of prayers of generalized confession and repentance.

When this is all done well, 'belongers' are very appreciative. They instinctively understand that there is possibly no other institution, building or officiant that can do what the Church does as well – though secular officiants are learning to use liturgical forms and create an appropriate atmosphere. The church funeral enables the expression of potentially strong emotions, such as grief, sorrow, anger, regret, relief, in a safe setting – the church building. It manages those emotions even as it makes possible remembrance, forgiveness, gratitude and, most gently, a looking forward to life without the deceased. All of this is possible through the traditional liturgies.

There is, however, a growing exception to what I have described. Some Anglican churches have been reluctant to make these accommodations. Funeral directors and the expanding profession of those who arrange funerals on behalf of the bereaved take note and steer mourners away from the Christian priest and towards the secular humanist officiant. The sense of belonging gets weaker.

Memorials

But one question is left hanging. How far can clergy go in seeking to be helpful to those who are not believers? Should we agree to take a non-religious service if asked? My own experience is probably typical of many clergy, even if the precise circumstances in which I had to think about this question were particular to me.

For a number of years I was a member of Sheffield City Council. Though I never sought the role of unofficial chaplain, occasionally colleagues treated me as such. Perhaps it was not surprising, therefore, when I was asked to officiate at a non-religious funeral service for a friend and fellow councillor, and then subsequently for the child of another. This places clergy in a difficult though not impossible position. After a great deal of agonizing, I agreed to take the services. However, I did so wearing a clerical collar and made it quite clear at the beginning of the ceremony that I was an Anglican priest though the service would not be religious. On each occasion the family also agreed that I could invite those who wanted to do so to join with me in prayer for the deceased towards the end of the service 'since there are those here for whom this is our way of taking our leave of those we love'. As long as everything is done with the agreement of the family and carefully explained, congregations accept that in a plural society such accommodations can be made.

What is more difficult, even if rarer, is a request for the church building to be used for a non-religious memorial or funeral service. This is more difficult because clergy will need to have the support of their church council and congregation. I have no direct experience of this. However, I note that in March 2012, the Dean and Chapter of Newcastle Cathedral made their building available for a humanist memorial service for Police Constable David Rathband, who had been shot dead while on duty. The Dean officiated and there was an address by a humanist speaker, as well as tributes from family and friends.

This is one further way in which in a plural society the Church continues the ministry of Jesus to those in need.

Witnesses to 'belonging'

I have probably said enough to indicate what I mean by instances of 'belonging', which I have distinguished from both attending (regularly) and believing. Many people will feel that they belong to the Church in the sense that they feel welcomed. They do not feel they are an intruder or the Church is an alien institution. They feel they can call upon the ministrations of the Church at particular moments of their life or the life of their communities. Some of them will also be believers, though not all and possibly not in any consistent or coherent way.

I now want to illustrate this idea of belonging further by invoking some witnesses who have put their thoughts into print. Each one illustrates something of what I mean. Some of what is said may surprise us if we are not attuned to the idea of 'belonging' without believing.

The journalists

One example is the journalist Jemima Lewis, a regular columnist with the *Sunday Telegraph*, who wrote recently about her religious convictions – or rather lack of them. She has a Roman Catholic background. However, she describes herself not as a lapsed Catholic, since Catholicism in a doctrinal sense never took root in her, but as a Catholic who does not and never has believed anything as far as the key dogmas of the faith are concerned, and sees no reason to attend regularly. Nevertheless, this does not stop her calling herself 'a good Catholic girl' or wanting her son baptized. She belongs, and she wants her child to belong as well.

But what does this belonging amount to? In what sense is she a Catholic? She tells us:

> I love being a Catholic. I love the exoticism and the familiarity of it: the cold clack-clack of footsteps on a church floor; the fluttering candles keeping alive the prayers of strangers; the tiny scrunched-up old ladies who can still be found, in the very highest churches, wearing black lace veils and murmuring along to the mysterious poetry of the Latin mass.[10]

There may be more here than Jemima Lewis acknowledges. I will return to this in the final section when I try to explain 'belonging' further in the light of all the examples, but for the moment we might ponder her words. Ms Lewis thinks she represents perhaps the majority of people in our society now, and I think she may be right. These are not so much the 15 per cent who said they had 'no religion' in the 2001 Census – they are more properly called 'atheists' – but many of the 72 per cent who ticked the box 'Christian' for want of some better description. The trouble with the Census and most opinion polling is that it does not allow us to make the further refinements we need to appreciate just what is happening in contemporary Britain. If we could drill down further into this majority we would be able to separate out two rather different groups – those who believe in a conventional sense and probably attend, and those who do not subscribe with much or any conviction to the creeds, and may or may not attend regularly, but would regard the disappearance of organized religion as a significant cultural and spiritual loss. Such people are found among all faiths – ones for whom, in Ms Lewis's words, 'conviction is not a prerequisite for worship . . . any more than worship is a prerequisite for religious identity'. They range from 'the secular Jew who gets his son circumcised . . . to the churchgoer for whom the smell of polished oak is half the attraction'. In other words, there is a group of under-researched people, whom I suspect are the really growing number, who are mainly outside congregational life, who want to see places of worship continue but who struggle as soon as theology is made too explicit.

Throughout the 1990s, the stories about Christianity that principally seemed to interest newspapers and magazines were those written by religion's detractors. Religion was attacked as delusion or a poison from which the nation and its children must be separated. But as I have already indicated, in more recent years these articles are being superseded by writing with a quite different theme – the *usefulness* of religion. Commentators generally begin by establishing their agnostic or atheistic credentials, but then go on to explain, sometimes in a half-embarrassed fashion, why they slip into cathedral evensong or take their children to carol services. One such, *The Guardian* columnist Simon Jenkins, stated rather boldly at the end of 2011 that churches were essential for 'maintaining our communal life'.[11] Writing just before Christmas he noted, and commended, the practice of many to become 'pray-for-a-day' worshippers who 'see in their church a repository of good neighbourliness without which the community would be poorer'. The Church of England in particular

> has a genuine talent for sustaining this communal centrality through thick and thin and mostly thin. This role in the local 'establishment' is far more plausible than the state version. Going to church at Christmas keeps alive a sense of what the Germans call *heimat* – an attachment to home, a refreshment of roots, an acknowledgement of continuity and tradition.

I think Jenkins may be wrong about state establishment and local establishment. They each reinforce the other. But the essential point is that unbelievers such as him can see real value in the ministry of the parish church. He goes on to say how he likes to visit churches – 'good places to sit and think'. Philip Larkin says the same in his poem 'Churchgoing'. Jenkins also recognizes that churches become more vital as centres of community life as the age of austerity collapses many other places where communal bonds were once forged. 'The parish church is thus the one building in any neighbourhood that is worth saving, together with God's acre, the churchyard.' Hard-pressed clergy, especially in rural areas, should take heart from these words.

The philosophers

But journalists have not been the only people commenting on religion's utility. Two contemporary, non-believing philosophers, Alain de Botton and Baroness Mary Warnock, have also spoken about their attitude towards religion in similar terms.

In 2012, the philosopher Alain de Botton published a widely reviewed book, *Religion for Atheists*. In it he acknowledged that once you set aside the matter of beliefs, there was a great deal to be said for religion. Religion had its uses, as the subtitle of the book made clear: *A non-believer's guide to the uses of religion*. This was an acknowledgement that far from religion poisoning everything, as Christopher Hitchens thought, it was actually rather good at providing crucial individual and social goods: fellowship, discipline and guidance, time for reflection, uplift for the human spirit, and so on. Society would be the worse for the lack of it. But that posed a serious dilemma for a nation in which increasing numbers had turned their backs on the Church, for in doing so they had also forfeited the benefits of organized religion. De Botton's solution, therefore, is to provide secular alternatives to the churches and all that goes on there. This was the secularist's equivalent of the Salvation Army's asking why the devil should have all the best tunes. Imitation, we should remember, is the sincerest form of flattery.

De Botton writes against a climate of growing uncertainty about some of the claims that were once made for the overthrow of revealed religion and its substitution by rational thinking and scientific progress. A more scientific, rational and religionless age does not seem to have resolved all moral dilemmas or led to better behaviour and happier people after all. De Botton, therefore, proposes to take all that he sees is good in religious practice and replicate it on a secular basis. So instead of the religious calendar there would be a secular equivalent designed to remind us of our good fortune and our responsibility towards others. Instead of churches there would be beautiful buildings where we could meet together and welcome the lonely, the lost and the stranger as brothers and sisters. Architecture and art, once at the service of religion, could be harnessed in the name of godlessness. Instead of Holy Communion, neighbours and strangers alike could meet together in Agape Restaurants around monastic-like communal tables to share food and conversation.[12] (It is a strange paradox that seventy years ago, Dietrich Bonhoeffer was arguing for God without religion, whereas today de Botton and others want religion without God!)

On the whole, reviewers were not sympathetic to de Botton's ideas. Some pointed out that this attempt to find a non-religious alternative to religion had been tried before: the French revolutionaries had a version, as did the French philosopher Auguste Comte. A more sympathetic reviewer, Jeanette Winterson, noted that this made a welcome change for anyone 'fed up of [*sic*] the Dawkins Delusion that rationality and science are the answer to the human condition', and commended de Botton for at least 'trying to do something about the frightening mess that we are in'.[13]

Another, somewhat surprising, witness to religious usefulness is the moral philosopher Baroness Mary Warnock. Yet in much of her recent writing she makes it clear that even convinced non-believers such as herself accept that the Church has a vital role to play in contemporary, secular society. I am not sure how kindly she would take to my classifying her as a 'belonger', but in my sense of belonging she clearly is.

In a recent book, *Dishonest to God*, which begins with a critique of the Church's stance on a number of urgent contemporary moral issues, Lady Warnock accepts that in a post-Christian society, the long-established rituals and ceremonies of organized religion may continue to play a valuable part in individual lives and in the lives of communities. This may be, she explains, at times of disaster or great moral perplexity. The ceremonies she has in mind include funeral and memorial services or more public occasions, such as a service of thanksgiving when a war is over. Churches and cathedrals have learnt over the years how to handle these occasions even though the congregations that assemble there consist of people of many beliefs and none. But 'such ceremonies are a bond, and an expression of shared emotion that society would be greatly worse without'. She then goes on to say something that other non-believers might be less willing to acknowledge:

> Moreover, some people at least, though they do not believe in a personal God watching over them, nevertheless sometimes need to behave as if there were such a being; their emotion may be a sense of a generalised gratitude, a generalised remorse, a generalised sense of pity and sorrow for the sufferings of others. For many such people, of whom I am one, the rituals and the metaphorical language of religion, their traditional religion, are the most accessible and the most fitting expression.[14]

There is no way that the more hard-edged atheists would want to admit to this utilitarian value of religion. But it echoes what we have found with the pastoral offices, and it underlines the 'tribal' aspect of Anglicanism that Lord Rees remarked upon. But if people like Lord Rees and Lady Warnock are to continue to feel that the rituals of the Church are able to include them – if they are to retain this sense of belonging – that will only be possible in a certain type of Church that articulates a certain type of theology.

Summary: the meaning of 'belonging'

We are now in a position to attempt a summary of what I think it means to say that many people in this country, perhaps even the majority, continue to 'belong' to the Christian Church and faith. What do our findings tell us?

The 'constituency' of those who belong consists of two principal groups. First, there is a large number of people who do not want to write off the Church or Christianity, but who are not, and may never be, church attenders in any regular way. In addition, although their own Christian beliefs may be unorthodox, incoherent, thin or tentative, they know that an explicit atheism does not do full justice to where they are in terms of beliefs and values, and that a society and culture without religion might not be desirable. This is why they call themselves Christians. There is also a second group of people who are non-believers but who also see value in organized religion and would regret the disappearance of churches. These people are much less likely to self-identify as Christians and some would positively resist such labelling. This latter group is probably the less understood of the two. But all of these I would call people who belong, with the first group belonging in a stronger and the latter in a weaker sense.

For those who belong, the Church and organized religion perform a number of functions and satisfy a number of needs. I will comment on three.

First, when people seek out the ministry of the Church, as individuals or as communities, they are bearing witness to the fact that for many people the Church remains the principal, if not the only, repository of meanings on specific occasions. When a child is born, a couple marry, a person dies or tragedy overwhelms a community, people feel a need to understand the significance of such events by setting them within some larger context of meaning than whatever meanings the individuals concerned may or may not bring. This is especially important when something happens that brings individuals and communities to a place where their own resources for making sense – intellectual, emotional and moral – seem to run out, such as the killings in Soham and Whitehaven. At these moments it becomes clear that very many people still 'belong' to the Christian faith and Church. These religious meanings can sometimes be buried deep within a culture and may even seem to have vanished altogether – until called upon in some hour of need. A number of commentators have noted the way in which Christianity had apparently been expunged in several countries in the old Soviet bloc, yet when those atheistic regimes began to falter, the Church and Christianity were called upon to supply alternative values and alternative meanings as well as places to meet.[15]

Second, the Church continues to articulate those deeply held values that communities – and the nation as a whole – share and that bind people together. Christianity – as mediated through the English churches – remains an influential source of community cohesion because it stands for and proclaims, and its followers practise, tolerance, neighbourliness, civility, compassion, repentance, forgiveness, reconciliation, love. For many people, living by these values is the heart of the Christian faith and more important than any doctrine – about which they may be very hazy. Commitment to these underlying virtues is hardly surprising since for the better part of four hundred years, the people of England have been trained in them through the influence of the Book of Common Prayer. One reading of the Prayer Book's Litany – which continues to be said as part of the Ash Wednesday liturgy – would make the point: it is an attempt to enlarge people's sympathies and bind people together. Praying the Litany is an exercise in charity in itself and, at one time, almost everyone in the country would have been frequently immersed in it:

That it may please thee to succour, help, and comfort, all that are in danger, necessity, and tribulation . . .

That it may please thee to preserve all that travel by land or by water, all women labouring of child, all sick persons, and young children; and to shew thy pity upon all prisoners and captives . . .

That it may please thee to defend, and provide for, the father-less children, and widows, and all that are desolate and oppressed;
We beseech thee to hear us, good Lord.

Reinforcing this was the collect for Quinquagesima – the Sunday next before Lent. It asked for the gift of charity, reminding worshippers that 'all our doings without charity are nothing worth' and, rather starkly, that without charity 'whosoever liveth is counted dead before thee'. It is apparent that the vast majority of people want to live by these values and believe the Christian faith and the Christian Church are an important source of them.

For at least a thousand years Christianity has given the people of these islands what all human beings and human societies fundamentally need to flourish – some framework of meaning in which all that they do can be set and understood, and ways to manage how we live together in community. Since the Reformation that framework of meaning and its outworking has been mediated by the national Church. The framework may be less visible than it was, but people seem to understand and accept that the institutional Church holds it in trust for the nation and enables it to be called upon when needed. When some moment of collective crisis or the need for celebration arises, the Church is turned to. It will have the language and the ritual necessary to express and manage grief, sorrow, repent-ance, reconciliation, a fresh start, celebration, joy. The Church is the guardian of meaning for individuals, for communities and for the country. It is this that enables the Church of England to remain 'by law established' and also to remain established in people's affections. But this status has to be earned afresh with each generation.

This brings us to the final area in which the Church, specifically the Church of England, and Christianity as mediated through that Church, are perceived to have social value. From its origins in the sixteenth century, the Church of England has been part of the fabric of English society and therefore part of its identity. This is one reason why people call themselves Christians when invited to tick a box in the National Census. As long as the Church of England remains the established Church or, if disestablished, continues to act as a Church for all the people of England, it will remain able to play a part in the shaping of identity. Of course, other cultural factors have also contributed towards the creation of national identity and will do so again in the future. The Church will continue to play a central role in shaping the future of English identity as long as it can find ways of accommodating the faith to new movements of the Spirit, where they are compatible with the gospel. For instance, the feminist movement has challenged Christianity to look again at its Scriptures, doctrines and practice and understand them in new ways. It has enabled the Church to 'discover' women in its texts where they had often been invisible; it has led to the ordination of women; it has led to a revaluing of the role of women of faith in the family, the workplace and public life. As long as the Church remains open to such possibilities it will find that people well beyond its usual Sunday attendances will continue to support and value it. In recent years, however, some Christians seem to have become anxious not to be at the forefront of new movements of the Spirit. This is in some contrast to the great moral and social reformers of the past – in this country, one thinks of Lord Shaftesbury with his passion to improve the working conditions of children, William Wilberforce leading the opposition to slavery, and elsewhere, Martin Luther King leading the Civil Rights Movement in the United States and Desmond Tutu taking a stand against apartheid in South Africa.

The Church, then, stands at something of a crossroads. It can remember its past as the Church to which many belonged even if they did not attend regularly or struggled to articulate what they believed, and it can continue along the same pathway. Or it can turn in a quite different direction where attendance and commitment to a set of prescribed beliefs become the only marks of a Christian.

Conclusion

At some point in the last few years – probably during the decade of evangelism – the Church began to focus its attention more and more on the question of belief and attendance. The assumption was that being religious was essentially about having beliefs – beliefs that you self-consciously referred to as you lived your daily life, especially at those moments where some moral choice had to be exercised. The 'real' Christian was the one who could articulate these beliefs fluently and with great conviction. This was an assumption that a certain type of zealous Christian shared with a certain type of zealous atheist. The atheist Richard Dawkins has always insisted that all those who define themselves as 'Christians' yet cannot give an account of Christian beliefs should lose their Christian status; they were not really Christians at all. An increasing number of observant Christians found themselves agreeing. But this led to all sorts of confusions. If people stopped attending, it was assumed that this was because they had stopped believing. At the same time, and partly as a consequence of the focus on beliefs, those who had never attended, or at least very infrequently, now began to be unsettled. Were they wrong in calling themselves Christians because they found it very difficult to articulate their Christian identity in terms of beliefs? Were they wrong in thinking of themselves as Christians if they had never accepted that this required regular attendance? A crisis was created – but not so much a crisis of believing as a crisis of belonging. Since the Church did not understand that many non-attenders 'belonged', even if their beliefs were inchoate or minimal or even non-existent, it failed to support or encourage them through these difficult years. More than that, by thinking only in terms of beliefs and attendance it gave the impression that it was not interested in, or had no time for, those who belonged but did not attend and whose beliefs were thin, less coherent, not orthodox or pretty non-existent. The Church lost many friends and allies during this period.

If we are to put this right, we need, therefore, to distinguish between not two possibilities – believing and attending – but three: believing, attending and belonging. This is important because amid the depressing statistics about attendance, there are some other important pieces of data that may be overlooked. Yet they give us pointers for the future, since they suggest that there may yet be a significant number of British people who have not (yet) stopped belonging. If we can catch the sense in which they 'belong' and do not confuse that with 'believing' (in a more intellectually worked-out fashion) or 'attending' (regularly), we may be able to help them.

Many lay Christians and parish priests will recognize the phenomena that I have outlined in this chapter that seem to point to the idea of 'belonging' as something that is not coterminous with either attending or believing. I have argued that belonging in this sense is more typical of the English, if not of all the British, than either attending or believing without attending. We could say, therefore, that the English belong but do not believe – at least not in a greatly coherent or orthodox way – nor do they regularly attend. The evangelistic task in contemporary Britain, therefore, is not so much a matter of primary evangelism – these are not people who know nothing of the Christian faith – but of helping to bring some of those who belong to a point where they might be able to say 'I believe', and having said it, to join us Sunday by Sunday. This requires real acts of imagination and sympathy on the part of both clergy and laity, and it means being prepared for the long haul. In the meantime, there is the ministry to those who belong and who may never commit themselves to regular churchgoing.

This conclusion raises two further questions. I will not comment on them at this point, but simply note them since they are important and will need further consideration at later stages. The questions are these:

- What sort of Church can sustain this sense of belonging?
- In what way is that ecclesiology being threatened?

But before we can answer those questions we must first consider the two other categories – attending and believing. Are they all that they seem?

2

Attending

———◆———

I am a committed – but I have to say vaguely practising – Church
of England Christian who will stand up for the values and
principles of my faith.

David Cameron, Prime Minister, in a speech marking
the King James Bible's four-hundredth anniversary year

The world is awash with formless religiosity, much of it flowing
through non-traditional channels.   *John Gray*

We are not a religiously observant nation – except when it counts.
John Canter, writing in The Guardian
as an atheist, is an author and scriptwriter

In the Introduction I made a distinction between belonging,
attending and believing, and sought to explain what I mean
by belonging as distinct from attending and believing. At
the end of that Introduction I asked whether attending and
believing were quite what they seemed. In this chapter I
want to take that further and say something about those
who do attend church. What do we know about them (us)?
Why do we attend? What does that suggest for the ongoing
mission of the Church, especially the Church of England?
By the end of the chapter I hope to have shown that again, as
with those who belong, there are attenders of different types
and our reasons for attending can be quite complex. But first,
I will make some observations about those who have stopped
attending.

The fall in church attendance

We have already noted that the British have been walking away from organized religion since the late 1950s. Church attendance spiked immediately after the Second World War and then fell dramatically throughout the 1960s and continued to fall in all subsequent decades. There is still little sign of this decline being arrested and the situation is now grave. One set of statistics for a more recent period will serve to make the general point. If we look at the average number of those attending Sunday services across all denominations in England, Scotland and Wales, we find a fall from 5,341,000 (or 9.6 per cent of the total population) in 1990 to 3,634,000 (6.0 per cent) in 2010.[1] This means, among other things, that the country is oversupplied with churches to a quite alarming extent. There are, for instance, 3.5 million places in Anglican churches alone, with fewer than 1 million Anglicans occupying them most Sundays.[2]

One factor in the decline is the ageing of congregations. This is happening at a much faster rate than among the population as a whole. But as churchgoers cease to attend through infirmity and old age, or die, they are not replaced in the same numbers by younger generations. If we then assume the same pattern of ageing and non-replacement in the next decade, the average attendance figure for all denominations by 2020 would be 2,838,000, which would be 4.5 per cent of the population.[3] That would be a significant milestone because, if the number of observant Christians were to drop to these low levels, the ability of the Church to influence the culture more generally would be fatally weakened.

The ageing of the Church does not necessarily mean that it will inevitably collapse in every place. There are congregations of mainly elderly people that steadily maintain numbers despite losing many each year through ageing and death. They do so by providing an ethos that is welcoming to older people, making up for those who can no longer attend or die with a new generation of older people. A common mistake of more inexperienced clergy when appointed to such a church is to find older members an embarrassment, insisting that the entire focus of the ministry should be on 'families' or 'young people'. A church that can be welcoming to older people may be just as numerically successful as a church of younger families, especially in those places to which many people choose to retire. However, as the demographics of a parish change, the church will want to look at how it can adapt to be able to welcome other age groups.

At the other end of the age spectrum the Church has generally struggled to bring in an equivalent number of younger people to replace those lost through frailty or death. Those young people who came from families of 'belongers' rather than attenders slipped through one particular net: the Sunday school. The collapse of Sunday schools has been especially dramatic. They were a feature of most young lives until the 1950s. It is probably true to say that even as late as 1957 more than three-quarters of the adult population had been through a Sunday school. Today the number is negligible. This has been a critical factor in eroding the general understanding of Christianity among those who still retain a sense of belonging. For a while, the Church relied on the day school to make up the deficiency of Christian knowledge that non-attendance at Sunday school created. But this became a vain hope after state school syllabuses were revised in the 1960s. Instruction in the Christian faith gave way to a more comparative-religious approach in which no one religion was privileged. It was possible for young people to leave school knowing as much or as little about Christianity as Islam. At the same time, the daily act of Christian worship became a more generalized and moralizing assembly so that young people had little or no experience of Christian worship either.

Why have the younger generations walked away? The reasons people give are many and various, but some generalizations are possible. In the early 1990s, for example, people in general, and young people in particular, gave 'boredom' as a principal reason for giving up regular attendance at church.[4] 'Boredom' could have referred to anything: dull and inappropriate sermons, lacklustre liturgy, a failure to involve people as readers or servers, competition from places of entertainment that used modern technology and music – and so on. There has also been the growth of what at one time was called 'the continental Sunday' – the retreat from Sunday as a day set apart or a day of rest – which gathered pace throughout the 1980s. There was a time – within the living memories of some people – when almost all weekday activities came to a halt on Sunday. In this respect, Britain was quite different from much of the rest of Europe. People's loyalties to their church were not put to the test by rival attractions and possibilities. Now people pursue leisure and recreational activities that take place on Sundays or that take them away from their home parishes. Parents of younger children often find that young people's football clubs and ballet lessons require them to act as taxi services on Sunday mornings as well as midweek. At any rate, people have been making their own decisions about leisure and recreation time and fitting Sunday observances around that, rather than the other way round.

During the period 1995–2005, people were more likely to give a different reason for non-attendance: they had stopped believing. In part this may reflect the sustained attack on Christian belief from the New Atheists during this time. The Church was slow in recognizing how unsettling this was for Christians of every generation, and how ordinary members of congregations needed help in understanding and responding to the charges. If my own household was in any way typical, parents especially were likely to face critical questions about their beliefs from young people who had read the very readable books of the scientist Richard Dawkins. But few clergy felt able to rebut the criticisms with confidence, not least because most clergy, along with much of the population, did not have much of a scientific education.

Finally we might notice one further major shift that occurred from about the 1980s onwards – the growing distinction people made between traditional religion and what came increasingly to be called 'spirituality'. Before the 1980s, spirituality was anchored exclusively in the churches where (male) clergy determined a person's spiritual journey. It was about drawing near to God through means prescribed by the Church. It was about the sacraments, the liturgy, set prayers – such as the rosary – and guided retreats. But as people walked away from organized religion they recognized that they remained spiritual beings with spiritual needs. They began to find their own resources. This was certainly true of many of those women who left the Church for good when they were young, but in middle age began to make a distinction between religion and 'spirituality'. Now some women set out on spiritual pilgrimages of their own. They began to interest themselves in alternative spiritual practices and techniques – from Buddhist meditation to goddess worship. Many of these techniques were 'holistic' in that they involved physical disciplines as much as activities of the mind or the cultivation of certain sensibilities. According to some observers, those participating in alternative spiritualities of this kind, men as well as women, had set in motion a 'spiritual revolution' as a result of which, in a decade or two, they would outnumber those attending churches.[5]

While numbers have been falling across the United Kingdom, the rate of decline and the pattern of church attendance has varied from country to country. Scotland has the highest percentage of its population attending, at almost 10 per cent in 2010. England and Wales had about the same – 5.7 per cent and 5.8 per cent respectively – though Wales has a faster rate of fall.[6] Within England, the area of the country where numbers hold up best is the South East. But in every county, attendances continue to fall. If the figures for 2010 are projected to

2020, only London would have more than 6 per cent of people attending, the direct result of inward migration and the church-going habits of the black population. I will say no more about the quantitative evidence but take as a given that overall, for the past fifty or so years, increasing numbers of people have not been participating in organized religion on any frequent basis.

There is no single reason for people deciding to leave the Church altogether. However, contrary to what is sometimes said, the outflow has been very sudden – since the late 1950s and so within a single lifetime – and so serious that we are justified in calling it a collapse. Some of the more critical factors are outside the capacity of the Church to influence directly. Nevertheless, the Church did not help itself; indeed, it often contributed to its own decline. The truth of this can be seen if we think about what happened to one group of people in particular during this period – younger women. The Church failed them, and continues to fail them, though without always understanding quite why or how, and that has had lasting damage. If we reflect on that failure we can also begin to see what I mean by the sense of 'belonging' and why it is important to recognize what 'belonging' is and how easily it can be undermined. We can also begin to see why once the sense of belonging is eroded, falls in attendance follow. What became of younger women in the Church after the 1960s illustrates the relationship between belonging and attending, and points to a further critical factor in church decline.

The Church and younger women: a cautionary tale

In his book with the rather arresting title, *The Death of Christian Britain*, Callum Brown shows how from the 1960s, younger women began to give up on the Church in increasing numbers.[7] While not accepting his major claim that the loss of women is the single most important factor in the decline of Christian attendance in contemporary Britain, we should take note of what Brown draws to our attention. For many women in that decade, Christianity seemed to have little or nothing to say to them. They were the first generation of women across all social classes who were beginning to turn their backs on lives that consisted only of the domestic round and childcare and to make their way in the workplace. The women needed help thinking through their place in a changing world; but the Church – which is to say the (male) clergy – continued to affirm the importance of conventional family life, with the implicit assumption that the roles of men and women would be, and ought to be, the same in the future as they had been in the past.

This understanding of the female role had been the Church's refrain from the beginning of the nineteenth century, at which time it began to reverse its previous appraisal of women and religion. From the Reformation until around 1800, women were seen as a threat to religion and the good governance of the household – Shakespeare's shrew who needed to be tamed.[8] But after 1800, the threat was perceived differently: piety and the family had more to fear from male vices – drunkenness, gambling and violence. In contrast, female virtues offered the possibility of redemption. It was men who needed taming, and this was to be accomplished through the softening influence of the woman in the home. As a result, religiosity was feminized. One way in which this showed itself was in the depiction of angels. Prior to this period, angels were invariably pictured as masculine – strong and muscular. But by the early Victorian period, as Brown noted, 'angels were virtuously feminine in form and increasingly shown in domestic confinement, no longer free to fly. Woman had become divine, but an angel now confined to the house.'[9] This was the 'Angel in the House' who Coventry Patmore celebrated in his long narrative poem of that title published in 1854 – an idealized portrait of wife and mother, based on his own adored wife, Emily.[10] The poem was published in 1854, but it only became widely read in the later part of the nineteenth century. From then and into much of the first half of the twentieth century, the term 'angel in the house' was used as a summary of how women should be – married, selfless, submissive to their husband and devoted to their children. In the poem, Patmore wrote this in a section he subtitled 'The Wife's Tragedy':

> Man must be pleased; but him to please
> Is woman's pleasure; down the gulf
> Of his condoled necessities
> She casts her best, she flings herself.
> How often flings for nought! . . .
> She loves with love that cannot tire;
> And when, ah woe, she loves alone,
> Through passionate duty love springs higher,
> As grass grows taller round a stone.

Virginia Woolf, commenting on the angel in the house in 1931, summed up the woman's selflessness in this way:

> She sacrificed herself daily. If there was chicken, she took the leg; if there was a draught, she sat in it – in short she was so constituted that she never had a mind or a wish of her own, but preferred to sympathize always with the minds and wishes of others.[11]

Although Woolf declared that one of her objects in life as a woman writer was to 'kill the angel in the house', I am quite sure that my own mother, who was married in 1938, was unconsciously influenced by the ideal, despite the fact that she also held down a full-time job. Indeed, the irony seems to have been that while women such as my mother were extensively recruited into the labour force throughout the war years as men went away to fight, afterwards they continued to see their principal role as lying in the domestic sphere, even though they might continue to work. By the time I first came to conduct weddings as a young priest in the late 1960s, the angel in the house still exercised a powerful, if unacknowledged, hold. For most people, this is what the Christian ideal of marriage was, and to be married according to the Book of Common Prayer was to step into that role. But it was being challenged.

During the later 1960s and the 1970s, the Church reckoned without the growing influence of the feminist movement – within its own ranks as well as in society more widely. Women increasingly wanted careers of their own and that required the sharing of childrearing and domestic chores, something that was completely absent from discourse about the angel in the house. However, this was not easy to achieve in either theory or practice: what happened when careers collided? Women wanted their voices to be heard and their opinions to count. Both women and men needed help in thinking about how relationships of greater equality could be made to work – in the workplace, within marriage. But this was rarely if ever the theme of sermons or church teaching or marriage preparation. The women who tried to juggle a job and motherhood, and who stayed in the Church, were often made to feel neglectful and guilty as preachers pressed on with traditional themes. Like Virginia Woolf, these women continued to feel the presence of the angel.

In addition, over the next few decades women's lives began to change in other ways too. Those who pursued careers delayed both marrying and having children. Some lived with partners and decided not to marry. Others stayed single. This has had a significant impact on subsequent demographics. According to the Office for National Statistics, by 2012 almost one-third of all households in Britain consisted of a single person.[12] While many of these were pensioners – something that would have been true in the 1970s – the growth has been in those aged 45–65. Some of these were the young women of the 1960s who entered into marriages that went sour and were not prepared to stay married once the children had left home. The Church's unrelenting message about marriage and the family could only make these women feel like wretched failures. Also, in so far as the Church had any opinion on other issues that directly affected women – matters such as contraception and abortion as well as a general understanding of male–female and same-sex relationships – it appeared unhelpful. From the 1960s, therefore, as women's place in the home, the workplace and in society generally began to change in the most fundamental respects, the Church seemed unable to contribute anything that might help women think about their role in the new circumstances of the times. It could only add to any sense of guilt they might have in abandoning a traditional role.

To some extent, the Church of England might have redeemed itself in women's eyes by opening the ordained ministry to them. Catholic Anglicans in particular should have understood where the (theo)logic of their understanding of priesthood was taking them in the context of the modern age. Priesthood is about making God findable. This is what priests are for: the Jewish priest in the Temple enabled sinful, Jewish worshippers to draw near to the Holy One through the shedding of animal blood in sacrifice; Jesus enabled Jew and Gentile to approach the Father through his own sacrificial life and death; the Church enables all people to find God through its proclamation of Christ in word and sacrament. This is in the first place the vocation of the whole Church, the royal priesthood. The Church makes God findable, and the God the Church makes findable is the God who in Christ took human flesh, came among us, died and rose again for all humanity, male and female. But the Church can only do this priestly work if it reflects these truths in its own being. 'Christ died for all humanity, male and female': a Church gathered for worship or active in the world that consisted solely of males would not be a faithful witness to the God who in Christ died for all. For this reason, it is essential for the Church to consist of male and female – as well as people of every race and language – if it is to help people find the God who died for all. If, as in the catholic understanding, the priesthood of the whole people of God can be focused in and represented by those ordained priest, they too must reflect those for whom Christ died – male and female – otherwise their witness is diminished and the gospel is diminished.

If the Church of England had spoken with one voice and joyfully ordained women, it would have signalled both that it understood the inclusive nature of the gospel and also that it was making a decisive shift from a patriarchal and sometimes misogynist past to an acceptance of male and female equality before God. It would also have enabled women to bring insights and influence to bear at every level of the Church's life. It would have ensured that the issues women (and men) were trying to deal with in the circumstances of modern Britain were addressed theologically. But the historic moment was not seized in that way. It became not an occasion for repentance, renewal and rejoicing, but the start of protracted internal conflict that only the most committed and determined women were prepared to endure. Not surprisingly, therefore, young women walked away from the churches in great numbers. This was a double, even a triple catastrophe, because as the women left they took with them their husbands and partners, and their children – the next generation. The women who left in the 1960s, 70s and 80s were confirmed in their belief who the Church was incapable of understanding its own gospel. Leaving seemed like a liberation. They saw little reason to return.

The Church believed that traditional Christianity could resist the cultural changes of the 1960s and that Christian women would not be affected by it. This was a mistake. The women were profoundly affected. This was not because they had capitulated to feminism or the contemporary Zeitgeist but because feminism and the Zeitgeist made them look again at the way they understood their own lives and faiths. It needed a serious conversation to take place in the Church if they were to stay within Christianity; but so often that did not happen. This is not to say that the women who left became atheists, though some did. Many simply lost interest in traditional religion.

The feminist insistence on male and female equality sent some women back to the foundation documents of the faith itself. They examined afresh biblical texts and Christian doctrine. The result was an epiphany. In many familiar passages, the presence of women had often been overlooked in the Church's teaching and preaching. They now became more visible. So, for example, references to women in the story of Christ's passion began to raise interesting questions. What exactly was their role? The impression can easily be given that the group surrounding Jesus was wholly male – until you take serious notice of the fact that many women also accompanied him from Galilee to Jerusalem, that women were present at the cross and at the tomb, even though the men had fled and given up, and that a woman was the first to proclaim that the crucified Christ was risen – although dismissed by the male disciples.

Women read texts and saw their relevance to issues such as the relationship between women and men, and the role of women and men in the family, in society and in the Church, in new ways and with a new significance. But many were alienated by the way in which the Church – as they saw it – brushed aside both their concerns and the need for all Christians to renew their thinking about these matters. Whatever their beliefs, however articulate or inarticulate they might be about them, they felt that the Church was no longer an institution that welcomed them – other than on its own terms. Even if they remained within the Church – as many clergy wives did out of loyalty to their husbands – they lost their affection and respect for it. They no longer felt the same affinity with it. In this sense they ceased to 'belong' because 'belonging' is first an attitude of mind and an impulse of the heart. It is not primarily about beliefs or attendance.

Areas of growth

There is some growth in attendance – though not enough to make up for the losses. Cathedral congregations experienced growth of 30 per cent between 2001 and 2011.[13] Adult numbers rose from 21,100 to 28,000 and child numbers from 5,700 to 6,800. In addition, the number of people volunteering in cathedrals rose by 24 per cent, with 14,500 offering their services in 2011. This represented 345 people for each cathedral. The bigger churches – those with more than 350 attending on Sundays – are also more likely to grow.[14] A church of this size probably indicates that it is Pentecostal or charismatic evangelical in worship and fairly or very conservative in its theology and ethics. It may also indicate that the minister is in his 30s rather than in his 50s. The age of the leader of the congregation seems to be a relevant factor – at any rate there is a correlation. Perhaps men – they are mainly men leading these congregations – in their 30s are still energetic and enthused, while those reaching their 50s are beginning to run out of steam. If this is the case, it ought to be something on which the Church's continuing ministerial education focuses: how are clergy to be re-energized at a certain point in their ministry?

The big unknown is the question of the relationship, if any, between church growth and church decline. Does a growing Church grow, at least in part, at the expense of other, smaller congregations? There is certainly anecdotal evidence. We know that people have less 'brand loyalty' than in the past. In the United States, a Pew Research Center survey found that 28 per cent of people had switched their religious allegiances during their lives.[15] In this country, clergy in some areas report that younger members of their congregations in particular have been attracted to the youth events of a larger, probably evangelical, congregation and have subsequently transferred their Sunday allegiance there, with parents sometimes following. Bigger churches can run many different types of midweek activity, often of high quality, which draw Christians away from their home parishes. Then the remaining congregation struggles even more. This is often the lament of clergy in rural areas within easy reach of a town or city. It is clearly something that the leadership of larger churches should be thoughtful about: can they contribute towards strengthening smaller churches and not simply hastening their collapse? If church leaders are serious about overall growth – which is not happening – they need to consider the possibility that their numerical success is someone else's numerical failure. The idea that the 'Spirit blows where he wills' can be used as an excuse to duck the question.

It also seems that midweek attendance in England is growing, even if slowly and from a very slim base. Of course, some of the 'midweekers' also attend on Sundays; but there are those who only come midweek. Overall, midweek attendances accounted for 0.6 per cent in 2010. This raised the total weekly attendance figure to 6.3 per cent in 2010. In the Roman Catholic Church, the availability of a Vigil Mass on Saturday evening has also proved popular. In some places the numbers attending on Saturday have threatened to exceed those who come on Sunday. In 2011, Philip Wilson, the Roman Catholic Archbishop of Adelaide, noticed another 'worrying' trend – the rising popularity of the 6 p.m. Sunday evening Mass.[16] In other words, more and more people want religious services at times that suit them and allow them to pursue various leisure and recreational activities over the weekend. The sense of belonging to one congregation is fragmented and Mass attendance becomes more a matter of individual resourcing.

In the light of these figures, the need for growing congregations is undeniable. But we should not talk about the re-evangelization of the nation until we have first understood at least some of the reasons why people have been lost and why regaining trust will not be easy. Nor should we be unmindful of those who do attend and the reasons they do.

Who attends – and why?

But what of those who do attend church? I have already noted that people tend to attend less regularly than they did. They also attend as a result of more deliberate personal choice rather than as a result of convention or social or family pressure. People come to church because they want to and because they think there are benefits to them in attending – though they are unlikely to put it in those terms. This is not necessarily a selfish decision or only a decision about oneself and one's own needs. A person may feel that through belonging to a congregation and participating in regular worship they are becoming part of a significant group for good in their community; they may want to be part of a 'family' that stretches round the world and embraces people of every race and language; they may want to meet and get to know others in their community who might value their friendship; and so on.

In a letter to a Sunday paper, one reader, Bob Holman, said this about his local church – and in doing so made it very clear why he attends. (The letter was written at a time when the Richard Dawkins Foundation had released the findings of an opinion poll that purported to show that Christian believing was waning.)

> I have just returned from our Sunday service at the Baptist church in Easterhouse, Glasgow. The congregation of 70 included teachers, care staff, office workers, two former drug users, the redundant and unemployed, two families from Nigeria and one from the Congo. The church receives no state grants, supports itself and also contributes to a doctor and midwife in West Africa, a couple in a deprived part of Italy, and helps send six youngsters to school and university in various places abroad. In my 25 years attending the church, I have seen it grow in numbers and add an extension that serves the community with youth activities and a drop-in centre. Our church is not rich in money, but it is rich in a sense of fellowship, sharing and social equality. We have no fear of 'militant atheists'.[17]

There are very few other groups meeting regularly in any place that bring such a cross-section of the community together or do the things this group of people do for the wider good.

So he and they come faithfully, Sunday by Sunday. But there is one pattern of attendance that seems to have escaped our notice altogether: those who come at particular times of the year and only at those times.

The People's Calendar

A few years ago one of my former students made an interesting observation. She was reflecting on the Church's liturgical calendar, the succession of great festivals and solemn commemorations that we keep and that over the course of 12 months remind us again of the key moments in the story of Jesus Christ and some of the principal doctrines of the Christian faith. What disturbed her was the undeniable fact that though some of these celebrations attract large numbers of worshippers, others do not, while some services that are not part of the liturgical year, in the sense that I have just described it, produce very large congregations indeed. Her conclusion was that we had in effect two liturgical calendars running in parallel, sometimes though not always overlapping. We called them the Church's Calendar and the People's Calendar (see Table 1).

The Church's Calendar starts with Advent and Christmas, moves through Epiphany to Ash Wednesday, Lent, Holy Week and Easter, and then Ascension, Pentecost and Trinity Sunday.

The People's Calendar is rather different. If we take the year beginning in September, and lay the People's Calendar alongside the Church's calendar, it begins a little ahead of that with Harvest Festival and Remembrance Sunday; then Christmas Carols and Christingle, Midnight Mass, Mothering Sunday, and Easter. At one time – until somewhere in the late 1950s – there would also have been a well-attended Watchnight service on New Year's Eve, but that seems to have disappeared now in almost every place. There may be particular local variations of this – such as an annual memorial service when the recently departed are remembered by name, which may be

Table 1: The liturgical year

Church's Calendar	People's Calendar
	Harvest Festival
	Remembrance Sunday
Advent	
	Christmas Carols
Christmas	Christingle
	Midnight Mass
Epiphany	
Ash Wednesday	
Lent	
	Mothering Sunday
Holy Week	
Easter	Easter
Ascension	
Pentecost	
Trinity	

at All Souls-tide or at Easter, or some remnant of the Whitsun processions in the North West or Bristol. In one of my own parishes, a very popular and successful service was 'Grandparents' Day'. Grandparents invited their grandchildren, and grandchildren their grandparents, to join them at the service, and the church was filled with drawings, letters and photographs that had passed between them. At the end there were balloons and lemonade for the younger children and sherry and cake for the adults. It was one of those occasions when three generations might be happily present. But whatever the occasion, the point is the same: the People's Calendar is not in all respects the same as the Church's. In fact it is quite instructive for every church to look back through its registers of services and construct its own People's Calendar by noting those occasions that consistently draw large numbers. (It is also interesting for clergy to ask how they divide their time and energy preparing for services on the different calendars.) We might wonder what we are to make of these two calendars.

There is a separate issue that arises from the fact that many congregations now find people attending less regularly because they travel and go on holiday more frequently than they did even a few years ago.

In 2011 I spoke to a conference of just over one hundred churchgoers drawn from a range of denominations. Most were over the age of fifty-five. I asked how many would be visiting relatives or friends or taking weekend breaks or holidays within the next six months, as part of a general pattern of the way they now live. Many hands were raised. A smaller number explained that they now spent a large part of the year in a second home; others said they were away on cruises or package holidays. They were anxious to say they attended worship – on the cruise ship, in the village where their other home was, and so on. The point I was trying to make was that they were not present in their home parish.

I will not pursue this further – other than to note it as an additional complication – but return to the matter of attendance according to the People's Calendar. We could, of course, become very anxious about what the democratic selection seems to suggest about the lineaments of faith of some people who attend worship only on those occasions. We might worry, for instance, that so many want to celebrate the Resurrection without first being in the upper room on Maundy Thursday or at the foot of the Cross on Good Friday. There may be a worry there, though I suspect it is overdone. Many of the themes of Holy Week are present at other times, not least in the narrative over bread and wine at every Eucharist and in hymns sung across the Christian year.

But leaving that issue to one side, it may be at least equally important that we try to figure out why the popular calendar takes the form it does and why people stubbornly refuse to bend to the exhortations of the clergy about the importance of coming to all the festivals and commemorations of the Church's liturgical year.

I would make three brief observations. First, many of the celebrations in the People's Calendar involve symbols or small rituals or bodily movement or all three. At Harvest people bring gifts and present them. On Remembrance Sunday, in my last church, at the end of the Eucharist, poppy wreaths were brought forward and laid at the war memorial in church and the congregation quietly filed out, placing their own poppies beside the wreaths. At Christmas carol services and memorials for the dead, candles are lit and carried. On Mothering Sunday there are posies of flowers. All this is a reminder that religion is not just about what goes on in our heads but what stirs the emotions – and that may come about through action and symbol as much as words. It is a rebuke to our often over-cerebral approach to liturgy and faith. Perhaps the best illustration of this is the children's Christingle. Most of what is communicated will be done through symbol and ritual actions – receiving the Christingle and passing on the light. Much of this speaks for itself and requires little interpretation. It has the power to interest, excite imaginations and move to worship. It will bring together and unite the generations. This is why, according to the Children's Society, in 2007–08, 6,518 such services were held for the Society alone, bringing 595,419 children and 537,735 adults into church – surely one of the most popular services the Church ever holds. In some places, there will be very few parents who will not have come to church at least once while their children are small.

Second, many of these celebrations and commemorations have as their focus some or other aspect of everyday living that is then set in the context of Christian faith. So, for example, the Harvest Festival is about thanksgiving to God for the food we eat and the flowers in which we delight, gratitude to those who grow them, and our responsibilities towards both the planet and those with whom we share it. On Remembrance Sunday we reflect on the fallen world in which we live and call to mind the sacrifices our forebears, brothers and sisters, children, friends and neighbours have made and are still asked to make on our behalf – a mix of profound gratitude and sorrow. And so on. The themes and focus of these services are often very personal, touching us at some of the most significant points of our lives – blessings and bereavements, perplexities and hopes. They allow us to have and show deep emotion – but in a managed way and in a safe place. It is hardly surprising, therefore, that people come in numbers.

Finally, these services can often bring together the different generations. One of the most moving Remembrance Day services I recall involved students from the local comprehensive school, who had been studying Nazism and the Second World War, coming to see some of their project work displayed round the walls of the church, as if they were stations of the cross, and laying their own wreath at the church's war memorial. Needless to say, they came with their grandparents as well as their parents. Similarly, grandparents are often included at Harvest Festivals, Christmas carol services and Christingles.

The lessons are obvious. Many people continue to have a sense of belonging to the Church and the Christian faith. This is because there are still moments in their lives when the Church speaks to their condition through the annual cycle of celebrations and commemorations. The services on the People's Calendar, therefore, need more attention from clergy, not less. They touch parts of people's lives that are of fundamental importance for daily living. They should encourage us to ask whether there are other aspects of life – blessings or sadnesses – that we have yet to capture liturgically. They witness to the fact of 'belonging'; for many of those who come on these occasions may never come regularly and they might struggle to express their beliefs coherently, but they would be deeply offended if their sense of belonging were to be challenged or rejected by the Church. It is why they self-identify as Christians in the Census and opinion polls – something the secularists as well as the more zealous Christians will always struggle to understand.

The People's Hymn Book

An integral part of the services of the People's Calendar is the People's Hymnody. All the services in the Calendar have particular hymns associated with them. This is a matter of both words and music. When the expected hymns are not part of a service, people feel disappointed and let down. Their sense of belonging is weakened. In the period after 1960 there were many clergy who, for example, attempted to influence the way people responded to Remembrance Day by refusing to allow the singing of certain hymns that they thought were too belligerent or tended to glorify war. 'O valiant hearts' is now almost never heard and 'I vow to thee my country' struggles to maintain a place.

For many people, perhaps most, their understanding of Christianity will come from the teaching captured in the hymn book rather than any other source. We should recognize this and realize how much is lost when the rich texts of more traditional hymns give way to so many contemporary worship songs. What better expression of the meaning of the Incarnation could one hope to find than these words from 'Hark, the herald angels sing', committed to memory as a result of being sung every year at the Christmas carol service:

> Veiled in flesh the Godhead see,
> Hail the incarnate Deity!
> Pleased as man with man to dwell,
> Jesus, our Immanuel . . .
>
> Mild he lays his glory by,
> Born that man no more may die;
> Born to raise the sons of earth,
> Born to give them second birth.

This is why the preference of many clergy for modern songs and choruses lets down those who belong. Contemporary spiritual songs tend to make the belonger too self-conscious with their persistent references to how 'I' feel and what this means to 'me'. (One of my students came across one song that had 17 references to 'I', 'me' and 'my' in it.) They are also often theologically less rich than traditional hymns, which is likely to lead to a further erosion of Christian teaching among belongers and, as a result, a further diminution of the Christian culture of England.

Many hymns are prayers of encouragement in living the Christian life in a difficult world. In her semi-autobiographical early work, *Oranges Are Not the Only Fruit*, Jeanette Winterson noted a favourite hymn of her mother from a Pentecostal hymn book of the 1960s. It captures exactly what I mean:

> Yield not to Temptation, for yielding is sin,
> Each Victory will help you some other to win.
> Fight manfully onwards, Dark Passions subdue,
> Look ever to Jesus, He will carry you through.[18]

We can also note the fact that Winterson remembered the hymn from her childhood.

We might wonder why people come year after year when they know that they will hear the same readings and sing the same hymns. But this is the whole point. They come in order to hear the same readings and sing the same hymns because repetition is essential for human beings, otherwise we so easily forget. People come to refresh their faith, reminding themselves again what is important in their lives and why. The People's Calendar with its rituals and hymns binds strangers together, builds up the sense of belonging and enables people to assimilate and renew Christian faith.

Roger Scruton has pointed out that the 'hymnal shows us the extent to which the English Church was not merely a religious institution, but the foundation of a genuine popular culture'.[19] We can see why the BBC TV programme *Songs of Praise* has such an enduring appeal for those who belong: it is another occasion on which their spirituality is refreshed. But the loss of the hymn book and its wholesale replacement in many, mainly evangelical churches with spiritual songs is not producing a new popular culture but a smaller, narrower, exclusive culture of Christians who are increasingly cutting themselves off from their non-attending neighbours, many of whom still want to belong.

The People's Prayer

One of the ways in which the Church has eroded the general sense of belonging to Christianity and the Church, and made attending a more hazardous experience, has been the various attempts to revise or modernize the Lord's Prayer. This was an example of how the good intentions of liturgists had unintended and disastrous consequences. This was the one prayer that at one time all people in the country would have known by heart. It was said in the traditional form at almost every Anglican service. It was thus the one prayer that individuals could recite whenever in life they felt in need of spiritual support. In wars and conflicts, in times of sorrow and sickness, when all people could do was to pray, the Our Father could be recited. The effect of introducing new versions into worship was first to disorientate the irregular attenders and then to embarrass them: instead of being able to join in the prayer unselfconsciously, it now became apparent that they could not say it without stumbling. It also suggested – correctly – that the Church had no interest in the spiritual needs of those who attended less frequently.

As the traditional version of the Lord's Prayer was succeeded by new revisions, schools often failed to keep up with the changes, or did not bother trying. As a result, the prayer disappeared completely from some schools, including many church schools, and new generations of young people left school without the prayer as a resource for their future lives. The old compact between the Church and those who belonged was being broken.

What attenders say

Regular attenders, along with belongers, have had to contend in recent years with a sustained attack on organized religion in general and Christian faith in particular. Aggressive atheists have ridiculed and condemned Christianity and churchgoing. In such a climate it became much harder to sustain the feeling that you belong to the Church, especially when the Church itself has not always understood the idea of belonging or that there are different types of attender – the irregular attenders with patterns of their own, those who come according to the People's Calendar and those who are attending most Sundays. The irregular attenders were on their own, condemned equally by regular churchgoers for not attending more often and by secularists for attending at all. However, in more recent years the climate has begun to change. After many years of aggressive denigration of Christianity and the Church by some academics, journalists and broadcasters, other commentators have begun to adopt a quite different tone. They have come to resent the strident atheism of some of the advocates of secularism, and their failure to discriminate between the attitudes and practice of the majority of Christians and those of a more conservative type. Some writers and cultural commentators have been provoked into revealing something of their own beliefs and practices. These have included attenders of two types – those who attend and believe and those who attend but do not believe. The Church of England contains both! I will comment on some of those who have put pen to paper in order to show how diverse are the people in many of our congregations.

Attenders who believe

One of those who attends and believes and was irritated by an outburst of the secularist Richard Dawkins was *The Times* columnist Giles Coren. Dawkins had tried to suggest that the number of 'real' Christians was considerably less than the 72 per cent who claimed to be such in the 2001 Census. In effect, Dawkins laid out his own criteria for being a 'true' Christian: you had to be able to give a coherent account of your Christian faith and subscribe to certain doctrines deemed by Dawkins to be essential. Since so many people in a poll he organized were unable to do some or any of this, he decided they had no right to call themselves Christians. Coren was stung into giving an account of his own faith and practice.

He began by saying 'I was born an Orthodox Jew' and went on to say that he was a 'churchgoing Jew' and, therefore, a 'Judaeo-Christian in its most literal sense'. However, this duality makes him reluctant to identify himself as 'Christian' on, for instance, Census returns. 'For every self-identifying Christian who does not attend on Sundays, there may well be a non-self-identifier who does. Or it may just be me.' He outlined how he came to be a member of the Church. It seems that his grandparents were Orthodox Jews in Central Europe, but his parents made a decision 'to drop every last vestige of the religion of their forefathers for the sake of making progress in a secular society'. They stopped attending the synagogue, and when his maternal grandfather died they gave up commemorating Passover in the home. He was now 'stripped of any hope of being Jewish'. He was sent to an English public school where his 'spiritual lack' was satisfied by worshipping 'a Jewish God according to Christian doctrine in the English language'. He became an unbaptized practising Anglican. He subsequently married in the Church of England and is present in church most, though not all, Sundays. Going to church is something he plans to do 'for the rest of my life'.[20]

Coren wrote in order to counter a number of claims being made by Dawkins and other secularists. First, some secularists have argued that children should not be brought up in their parents' faith. Coren, however, makes it clear that growing children have spiritual needs that remain unsatisfied if they are not enabled to share in some religious practices when young, and this usually means the practices of their parents. This is not indoctrination. Young people are not systematically being taught or trained to turn their backs on or despise other religions or the viewpoints of non-believers – something that is, in any case, hard to do with total success in a plural society. As young people become older they will make their own decisions and commitments. But the plural nature of contemporary Britain does mean that the religious identities of many people will not be quite as straightforward as the pollsters would imagine, even if they are regular attenders at a particular place of worship.

In the second place, Coren objected to the idea that someone should be able to claim the right to tell another person whether they were or were not a 'Christian' – and by extension a Jew or a Muslim. This was a matter of some importance and sensitivity to him because of his Jewish ancestry. The Nazis had once defined what it was to be a Jew. 'Historically,' he wrote, 'when people get to imposing their own definitions of religiosity on others, you're looking at persecutions.' We do not have to press this as far as Coren does to know that there is something disagreeable about that tendency to deny the appellation Christian to those who do not subscribe to some interested party's definition. But, of course, some Christians are inclined to do this as well as secularists.

Attenders who do not believe

Giles Coren, describing himself as a churchgoing Jew, illustrates the way in which the religious identity of attenders in a plural society is becoming more complex – and interesting. But the complexity is greater than this. We tend to assume that anyone who attends church regularly is at least a believer, however unconventional. It does not seem to make much sense to suppose that someone would come to church week by week even though they did not believe what the Church confessed in the creed. I think I first realized that this might not be true of everyone when I attended evensong at Sheffield Cathedral one Sunday following a return to the city after an absence of 25 years. I saw someone I had known when I had lived in Sheffield previously. I was puzzled because I had known him then as a convinced non-believer. At the end of the service I approached him and eventually expressed my puzzlement. 'I thought you were an agnostic,' I said. 'Yes, I am,' he said with some exasperation. 'But I'm an Anglican agnostic!' He went on to say that he often came to the evening service because the music moved him and the whole service provided an oasis for quiet reflection in a noisy and busy world. He was able to call at the cathedral because he could slip in and out anonymously. But, as he pointed out, there are very few churches now apart from cathedrals where this is possible. At any rate, meeting him alerted me to the possibility that others in congregations might be present for similar reasons.

Since that encounter, other non-believing attenders have made themselves known more publicly. The journalist Tim Lott, for example, is a non-believer, yet in 2010 he wrote an article in *The Times* in which he spoke about his journey from hostility towards the Church to attendance. He explained that as a child he had found the Church an 'outdated institution' for which he had no interest or enthusiasm. But when he and his wife had their first child, he found himself in his local Anglican church in order to secure a place for his daughter in the church primary school. 'I felt', he wrote, 'physically ill at being back on the pews', and did not return for a long time. But seven years later he was able to write about the 'surge of contentment' that suffuses him now on Sunday mornings when he attends church. He does not believe in any conventional sense, but he does 'take communion' and can 'barely think of a more satisfying way to spend an hour and a half on a Sunday morning'. He goes on:

I had not, in the years since I first walked into St Martin's Church, converted to Christianity. I was still as sceptical as ever – about Christ as our Saviour and Lord and his Father the almighty God. But I was converted to the church, which now I understand that, despite all its flaws, can be a real force for good in a community.

Of course, open agnostics of this type do need a tolerant version of the Christian faith to which they can relate. Not all churches will welcome someone on Lott's terms and not all versions of Sunday worship will be as comfortable for someone like him. But Tim Lott found what he needed in his Anglican parish church: 'I don't know when I started to appreciate the preciousness of that time when you could be alone with your thoughts and whatever definition of God you happened to bring with you.' And he does find some aspects of the regular liturgy helpful: 'The prayers offered at the end of each service that reach out to those who are bereaved or suffering, both in the parish and in the rest of the world, I find very touching.'[21]

Lott is clearly someone who is no longer hostile towards religion and is open to new experiences that may have a source in organized religion. So far, he has not looked back.

The distinguished political journalist and historian Anthony Howard, who died in December 2010, similarly attended quite regularly his parish church of St Mary Abbots, Kensington, although he was agnostic about God's existence. This was the church where his father had been a priest. He attended throughout his life 'out of custom' and 'an aesthetic appreciation of church services'. When his friend and former brother-in-law, the journalist Alan Watkins, died in May 2010 and the officiating priest failed to appear, Howard felt quite confident in leading the funeral service from the Book of Common Prayer. He exactly reversed what Grace Davie called 'believing without belonging': he did not believe in anything supernatural but did believe in organized religion and attended church. I would guess that open agnostics of this type are more numerous than we may think, though they tend to keep their heads down and are easily over-looked in those opinion poll surveys that force those questioned to opt for either the 'believer' or 'non-believer' category. The national Census of 2011 is also unlikely to reveal the extent of open agnosticism; indeed, it will probably hide it.

The significance of a congregation

Sometimes it is Christianity's sternest critics who provide the clues to understanding the significance of the things we do, including attending church and being a member of a congregation. Why are Christians seemingly so blind, so deaf? Part of the reason may be that as we have become more self-conscious about our Christian faith and the pressure on us all the time to justify Christian belief and practice in these more secular times, we are constantly casting round to find theological reasons for what we do. As we do so we overlook other accounts. So, for instance, I note that over many years of helping prepare men and women for ordination I have read numerous essays about the Church as the body of Christ. Paul's metaphor is striking, but it immediately focuses attention on one aspect of what it is to be a Christian congregation. The ordinands write about how we should rejoice in the different contributions each member makes, valuing each, despising no one, because the Church needs different people to play their parts if the whole body is to function well. I have very rarely read about the way in which a congregation brings together in a particular place people who might not otherwise meet other than casually, and how that makes an important contribution towards community cohesion. But it is this that Alain de Botton, the atheist philosopher, particularly noted when writing about what atheists can learn from religion. This is his account of what it means to be a regular attender at a Christian church – which is borne out by Bob Holman's letter that I quoted above:

The composition of a typical congregation at a service feels significant. Those in attendance tend not to be uniformly of the same age, race, profession or educational or income level; they are a random sampling of souls united only by their shared commitments to certain values. A service or mass actively breaks down the economic and status subgroups within which we normally operate, casting us into a wider sea of humanity. We are urged to overcome our provincialism and our tendency to be judgmental – and to make a sign of peace to whomever chance has placed on either side of us.[22]

The Times columnist Daniel Finkelstein wrote movingly in 2012 on this same theme, though from a Jewish perspective. He is a secular Jew, summing up his scepticism in this succinct but powerful observation: 'The idea that there is an all-seeing God who can find your missing dog if you pray to him, but somehow overlooked the Holocaust, does seem improbable.'[23]

Nevertheless, he wants to attend the principal rituals of the Jewish religion and to be part of the Jewish community even though he is quite unable to believe its supernatural claims. Why? He says that by attending those hallowed rituals of his Jewish ancestors he derives spiritual comfort and 'intellectual sustenance'. He goes on

It acts as a constant reminder that there is more to life than just us, that there were more people before us, and generations still to come. And those generations puzzled over the great questions of life and shared wisdom ... And by belonging to a religious community, I can ensure that my love of Mankind is also a love of Man, of real people.

Judaism is generous and has no difficulty in allowing secular Jews to participate in those rituals that continue to bind the Jewish people together. Historically the Church of England has been equally generous, agreeing with the first Queen Elizabeth that it did not want to make windows into people's souls. This is the Church that the contemporary emphasis on correct belief threatens to undermine.

The importance of the building

But attending requires the maintenance of parish churches. Here we strike another modern fashion. From time to time I hear both laity and clergy lamenting the fact that they have to put a great deal of effort into maintaining a building. This is regarded as time that could be better spent on doing some more direct evangelism or mission. I also note the way many 'fresh expressions' are about meeting in any sort of building rather than a church, as if a church building could only be of interest to those already committed. The objection to the church building is often reinforced by arguing that 'the church' is in any case not the building but 'the people'. This is one of those half-truths that is used to perpetuate something that is not true at all. It is true that in the New Testament 'the church' refers to the followers of Jesus in a particular place, meeting at that time in the bigger homes of the more wealthy Christians. But it is not true that the building itself cannot be a means of serving others and important in its own right.

Janice Turner, a non-believing journalist, made this confession in an article in *The Times*. It seems that just before Christmas 2011 she was shopping in Oxford Street, in central London, when she received a telephone call containing some grim news. She found the noise and garish stores suddenly too much and sought a quiet refuge in the only place where she could sit and be still – a church, St Giles-in-the-Fields. 'A lifelong non-believer, a former rowdy teenage atheist, I drank in the peace and left restored.'[24] Reflecting on this experience she first of all realized that, while intellectually she might be in the same place as Richard Dawkins and the New Atheists, nevertheless her 'soul has needs that science alone cannot address'. But this creates a difficulty:

Where would the atheist firebrands have me go to feel sad, reflect upon loss and the savage unrelenting passage of time? A science museum maybe; an art gallery; a psychotherapist's couch; under a night sky, marvelling at the infinity of the cosmos? All have their appeal but none would have that church's mystery.[25]

But 'mystery' was not something she ever thought she would need. (Nor is it the first thing that comes to mind when entering the buildings so beloved of the fresh expressions pioneers. For them, the less like a church the building looks the better.) The point about older parish churches of whatever century is that they are able to speak about God, and to do so in many different ways. Their dark corners and hidden recesses evoke the sense that God is always going to be beyond our total grasp, that there is always more to discover and to know. Their beauty lifts our spirits and enables us to feel, like Wordsworth at Tintern Abbey, that 'presence that disturbs me with the sense of elevated thoughts'.

Turner noted that in his book, *Religion for Atheists*, Alain de Botton acknowledges the part that a building can play in soothing the troubled breast or uplifting the spirit. However, she rejects his solution for non-believers – that they should build alternative, non-religious, temples of rationalism to emulate the awe and wonder of churches.

> Why bother when in every other street there is a lovely and mysterious place like St Giles-in-the-Fields, where it is perfectly possible to reply to the question 'Is there a God?' with the only truthful answer: I do not know.[26]

John Gray, also commenting on de Botton's book, makes the same point:

> Rather than trying to invent another religion, open-minded atheists should appreciate the genuine religions that exist already. London is full of sites – churches, synagogues, mosques and other places of worship – that are evocative of something beyond the human world.[27]

My guess would be that the response of Janice Turner and John Gray is more likely to resonate with the majority of people than de Botton's attempt to provide wholly secular alternatives to religious buildings and rituals.

I have always regarded it as my first duty when appointed to a parish to ensure that the building is open every day and a visitors' book provided to record at least the presence of some people who visit and the reasons they come. Over the years I have learnt not to be surprised at the number of visitors and how important the open church has been for them. Sometimes, as with Janice Turner, people have just been grateful to find somewhere they can stop, sit and think for a while, often at moments of sudden crisis or sadness. Because many of life's significant moments are associated with churches – marriages, christenings, funerals – they become places of memory and reflection. Many who come are those who retain the sense of belonging though they are far from being regular church attenders. Although the reasons people give for entering the building are very diverse, as I look back over many years of chance meetings with people on these occasions, one stands out above all: the way a church building affords people an opportunity to think about those they have loved but have now lost in death. Perhaps this is not surprising, because many churches confront us with the presence of the dead all the time through their memorialization in tablets, tombs and stained glass. Every church distils this store of human sorrows and this provokes in those who sit there deep reflection. The poet Philip Larkin, who tells us in his poem 'Church Going' that he often liked to drop into churches, called them serious houses on serious earth, not least because the dead were buried and remembered there.[28]

In his autobiography, *Leaving Alexandria*, Richard Holloway, the former Bishop of Edinburgh, reflects on the importance for people of the open churches:

They are a haven for the homeless woman whose destitution is obvious, muttering to herself over there in the back pew; but they also accept the moral destitution of the confident man sitting in the dark chapel, gazing at the white star of the sanctuary lamp, heavy with the knowledge of the compulsions that have dominated his life and refuse to leave him. Here both are accepted in their helplessness. There is no reproach. Churches do not speak; they listen. Clergy speak, unstoppably.

He goes on to say that Church buildings that stay open 'know better' because 'they understand helplessness and the weariness of failure, and have for centuries absorbed them into the mercy of their silence'.[29] But where do such people go when the churches are locked?

Conclusion

I have been a priest for many years in parishes in urban, rural and market town settings. That experience leads me to two broad conclusions.

First, the pattern of attending today is quite different from the pattern I recall from my first days as a young priest. Today, people use the services more as a personal spiritual resource, to be accessed as and when they feel the need, and hardly ever as an obligation entailed by Christian discipleship. As a result, individuals develop their own habits of attending, and these may be frequent or infrequent, regular or irregular. They may follow the Church's Calendar or the People's Calendar or pick and choose as they think helpful. They would, however, be affronted if the clergy or anyone else were to suggest that they were not 'committed' Christians because they were not in the pews every Sunday.

Second, the number who struggle with doubts or find it hard to hold to all the doctrines of orthodox Christianity are far more numerous within our congregations than we might think. I have no way of knowing exactly how true that is, though if it is, we ought not to be surprised given the relentless squeeze that there has been on religious belief and church commitment for the past forty or so years. But Giles Coren, Tim Lott, Anthony Howard, Janice Turner and Philip Larkin alert us to the fact that people still attend church or use the church building for many reasons, sometimes because of their faith and sometimes despite having none. Attending may indicate believing or it may not. But if the Church of England makes it increasingly difficult and uncomfortable for people to attend irregularly or on any other basis than being a Sunday attender, it will break with its historic compact with the English people and become a wholly different Church. For most people that will make the Church of England a Church they have lost.

3

Believing

———•◦•———

Belief is like love; it does not allow itself to be forced.

Schopenhauer

In the beginning was the deed.   *Goethe*, Faust

He is an Anglican and latterly a Quaker, which he says provides a 'sense of absolute equality', and there is a degree to which faith has shaped and sustained him. But he has no interest in what he regards as institutionalised religion's 'dogmas and doctrines'.

Terry Waite interviewed by Mary O'Hara,
The Guardian, *15 November 2011*

Far from being its major weakness, doubt is the Church of England's most attractive quality . . . modesty, distaste for pros- elytising, or indeed any firm conviction that it is the only true faith, always restrains the C of E from such trash-talking.

Janice Turner, The Times *columnist*

Throughout this book I have been making a distinction between belonging, attending and believing – though there has been a great deal of overlapping. In this chapter I want to focus on believing, though inevitably it will also touch on questions of belonging and attending. I want first to consider the part played by beliefs in the life of many if not most of those who identify themselves as Christian, and then ask what is happening to believing at the beginning of the twenty-first century.

Beliefs and religion

I begin with a caveat. The idea that for most people religion is primarily a matter of beliefs is simply not true. The obsession with beliefs is a contemporary aberration. It is a mistaken idea of the period in which we live, due in large measure to three factors.

First, the emphasis on beliefs is a consequence of our most recent history. We can see how this came about if we think about British society and its engagement with religion since the Second World War. Immediately after the war there was a continuation and reassertion of traditional religious belief and practice. We noted in the previous chapter that until the late 1950s there was even something of a resurgence of attendance. Those who grew up at that time will remember the country as essentially mono-ethnic, mono-cultural and mono-faith. This was the last generation where Orwell's old maids bicycled to Holy Communion. There was little to cause British people to examine their Christian beliefs. On the contrary, it was widely thought that the war had been fought for the sake of Christian civilization. That was how Winston Churchill, the wartime Prime Minister, had expressed it, even though he was not himself an enthusiast for churchgoing.[1] It was also during this period that the Church of England ceded much of its power and influence to the state with the creation of what Archbishop William Temple called the 'welfare state'. This seemed to Temple the way in which in a modern, industrial society Christians could obey the injunction to love our neighbour. By cheerfully paying taxes we enabled government to provide universal education, a national health service, benefits and pensions – care from the cradle to the grave. In order for this to happen successfully the Church had to hand over to the state many valuable assets – hospitals, schools and personnel. In doing so it sacrificed more than resources: it became midwife to the creation of a secular religion – the NHS – and a secular priesthood – the medical profession.[2] It has often been said that the National Health Service is the nearest the British ever get to a religion. But in helping to create the NHS, the Church also surrendered much of its own social usefulness.

By the mid 1960s, Britain was coming to terms with a new reality: we were no longer mono but multi – multi-ethnic, multi-cultural and multi-faith, principally as a result of inward migration, a legacy of empire. As migrant workers settled and brought their families here, what began as a transitory population of people in search of work became settled minority communities. Today, cities such as Birmingham and Leicester will soon be places where the ethnic minorities are the majority. By and large, and with the exception of those from the Caribbean and parts of Africa, the ethnic minorities were mainly adherents of non-Christian religions. Mosques, gurdwaras and temples appeared in city streets alongside churches and chapels. As this happened, the original host community began to take a serious interest in what those of other faiths – Islam, Hinduism, Sikhism, Buddhism – believed. Other differences – the food people ate, the way they dressed, the languages they spoke – were thought to be cultural rather than religious, since not all Muslims wore the hijab and Indian Christians ate curry. The crucial difference between religious groups was what they each believed. So the question of belief came to the fore.

The second factor that has led to a concentration on beliefs is the result of what some have called the 'culture wars' between Christian apologists and advocates of secular humanism – the New Atheists – in the first decades of the new century. There had been nothing like this since Victorian society divided over Darwin's *Origin of Species*. Much of the contemporary attack on Christianity was conducted in print by those for whom words and ideas are important – academics, theologians, journalists, commentators. Perhaps inevitably, therefore, there was a tendency by those who spend their working lives in their heads and deal in words to exaggerate the role of beliefs and theology and underestimate the place of practice and performance in the lives of most people. This was very well illustrated in early 2012 when a spat occurred between Professor Richard Dawkins, the high priest of New Atheism, and his Christian opponents. Dawkins commissioned through a Foundation he had set up a poll from IPSOS/MORI on the place of religion in the lives of the British people.[3] The poll found – in contrast to the 2001 Census – that less than half the population designated themselves as religious. Among those who self-identified as Christians, the research discovered that many did not believe what the Foundation regarded as key Christian doctrines – such as the divine Sonship of Jesus or his 'physical resurrection'. This led Dawkins to say that these self-identifying Christians were not entitled to call themselves Christians at all. In other words, they failed his test for what a Christian was: they did not hold to certain beliefs. The exercise was open to many challenges and as a piece of research was not particularly illuminating. But what was noticeable was the attempt to make being a Christian primarily a matter of *believing*. Of course, some Christians would not seek to challenge this because they too hold that being a Christian is essentially about holding correct beliefs.

In the third place, the tendency to highlight beliefs was a feature of much of the work of those who studied religion professionally in universities and colleges. From the 1970s onwards, departments of theology began to shift their focus from traditional Christian theological subjects – biblical languages and exegesis, philosophy of religion, church history and doctrine – to the study of all religions. Inevitably, religious studies explored what the different faiths believed. There was also a largely unacknowledged external pressure to do this from government – this knowledge was potentially 'useful'. It was useful, for example, when government worried about what was happening to British values and identity as society became more multicultural, and, after 9/11 and 7/7, when it worried about the religious narratives that motivated Islamic terrorists. All of this helped to safeguard the subject when utility and relevance became critical factors for universities to judge whether particular areas of study should be retained or not. A great deal of information was amassed about institutional religion, including what people did and did not believe. It all led to an unconscious tendency to assume that religion is mainly about what people believe – what they hold in their heads and recite in their creeds and confessions week by week.

It is true that creeds and confessions are embodied in worship, and all Christians will want to know that a rational case can be made for the faith. It is also true that some people do find their way to Christ by exercising their reason – just as the wise men get to the manger through calculation rather than revelation. Yet for many ordinary worshippers – belongers and attenders – Christianity is primarily about the heart and the will; it is an emotional and practical matter before it is something cerebral – if it ever is. It is about going to church, receiving the sacrament, lighting a candle, holding a rosary or crucifix, reading the Bible, saying prayers, being part of a fellowship. It is about feeling close to God. In recent years, many have preferred to speak about their 'spirituality' rather than their religion. It is their practices rather than beliefs that are central to their lives. Even if they go to church, their spirituality may include rituals and practices unrelated to church-going, such as walks in the countryside, listening to music, lighting incense sticks and meditating at home. It also involves being a loving partner or parent, being a good neighbour and conscientious citizen, giving of one's best as an employee, being honest in business ... We could go on. In other words, for very many people, Christianity is about certain rituals and practices and above all an ethical way of living before it is about doctrines or propositions. This is why when people answer questions about their beliefs they may be rather hazy or understand them as questions about behaviour: 'Are you a Christian?' is taken to mean, 'Are you a moral person?' or 'Are you a good father?' – which is why polls that show that self-designated Christians often have a poor grasp of formal doctrine in themselves tell us very little. Christianity, in other words, is as much a culture as a set of beliefs.

A vivid example of this is given by Richard Holloway in his autobiography, *Leaving Alexandria*. He writes about a woman he encountered in the 1960s when he was a priest in the Gorbals. Lilias Graham typifies the sort of person for whom Christianity is about how one lives as much as – or perhaps even more than – what one believes. She came from a privileged background, had gone to live in a slum tenement as a diocesan welfare worker – with the blessing of the episcopal Bishop of Glasgow. She devoted her life to her neighbours. Her flat was often filled with children, the Auld Hens women's group met there each week, she ran nurseries and youth groups and 'there was a constant flow of callers to her famous red door'. She became a local celebrity. The *Daily Record* called her 'the angel of the Gorbals'.[4] But Holloway writes that she found no need to 'theologise' and 'darken everything with thought'. Her relationship with the Church was one of 'affectionate toleration'. She liked going to church but 'not too often and never for too long'.

> She enjoyed the quiet rituals of the Christian year. She was the only person I knew who decorated her Christmas tree with real candles, a tradition she'd learned in Austria. She liked these practices because they added grace and beauty to life. The poetry of quiet religion appealed to her. The doctrinal obsessions of noisy religion bored her.[5]

None of this should surprise us. What draws most people to faith in the first place is probably the fact that it enables them to live their lives better – and this is as true for those who join churches where holding correct belief is stressed, as for those who attend churches that rather leave people to their own theological devices. Each of the world's monotheistic faiths – Judaism, Christianity and Islam – affirms everyday life and has given adherents the skills needed for living it. The faiths do not call people out of the world or teach them to turn their backs on it. (I say this despite strong traditions of asceticism in Catholic Christianity – though not in most of Protestantism and not at all in Judaism or Islam.) Ordinary life is not repudiated, for God is to be found there – the meaning of the Incarnation. Christianity influences lives as much by what it celebrates as what it teaches and preaches. At the heart of the Church's life is the celebration and so sanctification of ordinary life, including family life, life in the community and at work. All this is what makes people Christians or holds them in the faith. Belief has its place; but we should not exaggerate the role it plays for many people.

Of course, it is true that at particular moments in Christian history, the question of correct belief assumed greater significance. At those times, even ordinary Christians might have been more doctrine conscious. These would include periods when heresies had to be combated, or when another faith challenged, or when the Church itself became divided, as at the Reformation. But for the most part, Christians were content to practise the faith and leave theology to the theologians. The present time is no exception, though teaching the faith at a time when we are very conscious of other faiths and when the voices of unbelievers have been especially strident, has assumed a greater priority for clergy and lay leaders. But this should not mislead us into thinking that for most Christians, most of the time, the question of beliefs preoccupies them. It does not.

Context of believing

However, over this period – roughly from the end of the 1950s – the circumstances in which people believe in contemporary Britain have been changing. In two respects in particular these changes have had huge implications for believing. First, we have moved from being a culture in which religious belief was taken for granted to one where this is no longer the case. In a religious culture – as the psalmist tells us – it is only the fool who says in his heart there is no God and who has to justify himself (Psalms 14.1; 53.1). But now the tables have been turned and it is the believer who has to justify himself in this more secular and indifferent climate. Second, belief is no longer something that is simply handed down from one generation to another. In contemporary western societies, including Britain, we forge our own understandings and sit lightly to traditional teaching unless and until we have made it our own. I will briefly trace both of these developments before commenting further.

Beliefs under pressure

In 1962, a group of Cambridge theologians published a volume of essays entitled *Soundings*.[6] It was a first sign after the war that Christian belief was once again coming under enormous pressures. They wrote the book because they feared that the theological world of the time was in a dangerous state of complacency. Christian faith was facing challenges of which it was scarcely aware. So, for example, John Habgood, a scientist who would later become Archbishop of York, wrote about the widely accepted belief that there was now a truce between science and religion whereas, in his view, 'all is not well'.[7] In fact what Habgood feared turned out to be something of an understatement. In the following years religion was to face attack both from those reviving older challenges from science – cosmology and evolution – and those pressing hard the implications, as they saw them, of new areas of scientific research, such as neuroscience and genetics. *Soundings* was prophetic; yet despite the warnings it contained, it failed to create the sense of urgency the Church needed. On the contrary, in many respects the 1960s seemed to be a time for some optimism about the future of the Church.

This was a time of growing prosperity following the privations of the war and immediate post-war period. It was also a time of social upheaval and change as a younger generation began to throw off the more restrictive form of life of more traditional society. It was the birth of individualism, sex – sexual intercourse began in 1963 according to Philip Larkin – drugs and rock and roll. Christians needed support and encouragement in understanding what was happening. They needed Christianity to be articulated in ways that would speak to the new age. They looked expectantly to the Church and the clergy. Some clergy believed that traditional expressions of Christianity had become a barrier that had to be overcome. Attempts were made to restate aspects of Christian belief – such as Bishop John Robinson's work of popular theology, *Honest to God*, published in 1963. That book especially provoked huge interest – it became a best-seller – and ignited a great debate about Christianity and the modern world that went far beyond the Churches.[8] Robinson drew extensively on other writers, notably Paul Tillich and Dietrich Bonhoeffer. From Tillich he took the idea that God should not be understood as 'out there' or above and beyond humanity but as the very 'ground of our being'. From Bonhoeffer's prison writings he was especially beguiled by brief and enigmatic references to 'religionless Christianity'.[9] According to the new thinking that Robinson both captured and inspired, Christ was to be found not in the churches but in the 'secular city' and the faces of the poor. This was the burden of much popular theology, and many books and articles appeared with 'secular' somewhere in the title – such as Paul van Buren's *The Secular Meaning of the Gospel* (1963), Harvey Cox's *The Secular City* (1966) and John Vincent's *Secular Christ* (1968). There emerged what was sometimes called 'South Bank' theology. The reference was to the fact that many of the leading exponents of this way of thinking in Britain were associated with Southwark Cathedral and other London churches south of the River Thames.[10] Finally, we came to what seemed to many the logical conclusion of religionless and secular theology – the idea of the death of God.

At any rate, it seemed an exciting, challenging time to be a young Christian, ordained or lay.

I remember this period well. In the later 1960s I was an undergraduate reading theology at Cambridge. It was exhilarating to find fellow students from other disciplines wanting to talk about your subject and the issues Robinson, Tillich and Bonhoeffer raised. Robinson was invited to write a full-page article in *The Observer* – 'Our image of God must go'. The Cambridge Divinity Faculty put on open lectures that attracted hundreds – subsequently published as *Objections to Christian Belief*. It seemed as if we were on the threshold of a golden age of great promise for Christianity in Britain. What better time to be an ordinand, a priest, a Christian! The irony of the situation – the idea of religionless Christianity or the death of God led by those whose whole livelihood depended on organized religion flourishing – was lost on us at the time and only dawned on us gradually. In the event, the reality that began to unfold was very different from what we envisaged. This was not the beginning of some new, radical and exciting form of public theology, but the last time in my lifetime that the Church was able to generate a serious public debate on theological issues. Paradoxically, after that only the New Atheists, by attacking theology, could keep it alive in the public arena.

Many of those who espoused these new approaches also warmed to a new way of doing theology that was beginning in Central and South America at the end of the 1960s and gradually finding its way to Europe – liberation theology. Liberation theologians, Catholic and Protestant, influenced by socialist and Marxist political thought, saw the heart of Christianity as a commitment to society's most deprived. This, they believed, was central to the ministry of Jesus and reflected God's own concern to liberate all who were oppressed, as he had once liberated the Israelites from slavery in Egypt. God had a 'bias to the poor'. Liberation theology encouraged a particular way of reading Scripture: Christians first examined their contemporary context, noting where the poor were oppressed, and then looked for similar situations or 'paradigms' in Scripture where God had acted for the poor; this in turn suggested appropriate ways of acting in the present. It was this theology that indirectly influenced some of the working assumptions of one of the Church of England's most influential reports of the last 25 years, *Faith in the City*.[11] The report – I was one of its authors – reflected on the state of Church and Nation following inner-city riots in 1981. One unintended consequence was that it encouraged a younger generation of Anglican priests, anxious to recover social relevance for the Church, to reinterpret their ministry as a form of community work.[12] Not all the laity were persuaded.

However, the radical theology from the time of *Honest to God* was not the theology that endured. How could it? It turned its back on church buildings, traditional liturgies and cultic practices. Christ was not to be found there, where the God invoked was the 'God out there'; Christ was already present in secular life and only needed to be named. But clergy soon realized that without sacred places and congregations of faithful worshippers, the Christian memory would be lost. The majority of lay people never doubted that for one moment, so perhaps it is not surprising that most of them remained quite traditional in their beliefs, although they did want them to be restated in a way that met contemporary criticisms. They turned not to radical theologians or clergy but to a lay apologist, C. S. Lewis, an Oxford English don, and an American evangelist, Dr Billy Graham.

Lewis had come to the notice of the general public as a result of some wartime broadcasts he made on Christianity between 1941 and 1944. The talks were published in 1952 as *Mere Christianity*. Although Lewis was an Anglican, he was also Irish and had witnessed in his earlier life the bitterness of Protestant and Catholic division. Perhaps this explains why he was at pains to set out what was in effect a non-denominational approach to Christian understanding. Lewis was also a convert to Christianity from atheism, and this too informed his writing. He knew from his own experience that the culture of the twentieth century did not make it easy for anyone to believe. *Mere Christianity* was an attempt to present the Christian faith in ways that both met modern criticisms yet made clear where Christianity parted company from many common assumptions of a more secular age. It was a confident statement and could be read approvingly by any part of the Christian constituency. His books – which also included *The Problem of Pain* and *Miracles* – have been in print ever since.

Billy Graham, an evangelical, who had held many large rallies in the United States in the post-war period, embarked on Mission England in 1984. Thousands came to his rallies and responded to his call to come forward and commit themselves to Christ. His preaching galvanized Christians of all denominations, and a substantial number of young men who were converted at his rallies subsequently became ministers and priests in the Methodist, Baptist and Anglican churches. Not all remained evangelicals.

But by the early 1990s, whether Christians read conservative or more radical theologians, it was becoming clear that belief was no longer something that came easily to people in a non-religious age. In the end, it was as a new generation of atheist critics began a concerted assault on religious beliefs of all kinds that the extent of the struggle people faced became apparent, especially after the publication in 2006 of Richard Dawkins's book, *The God Delusion*. This has been a very influential anti-religious tract. By 2010 it had sold over 2 million copies and had been translated into 31 languages.

What has been revealed, however, is not a straightforward decline of religious belief but a mixed picture. There has been decline as measured by churchgoing but this by itself is not conclusive evidence since people may still believe even if they do not attend – as Grace Davie maintained when she said the British were 'believing without belonging'. But the walking away from places of worship also points not to religion's decline but to its change and adaptation. As we have already noted, people started to make a distinction between spirituality and religion. Some of those who stopped going to church did not cease to be 'spiritual' people. They no longer thought of churches as the only places where spiritual experiences were to be had or the soul nourished. The move from religious observance to the pursuit of spiritual experience also signals a move from being overly concerned about beliefs to having more of an interest in 'experiences' – emotion rather than intellect. One is bound to say that much of this experiential activity turns out to be rather fleeting and somewhat shallow – as evidenced by the way people move from one spiritual technique to another.

The first change in the context of believing, as this brief review of the period since the war shows, is the pressure that religious beliefs have been put under. This is no longer a culture in which Christian beliefs are taken for granted. Believers have to be clearer about what they do believe, and to justify that both to themselves and, sometimes, to others.

But there is a further aspect to the context in which believers now find themselves.

Believing 'my way'

Among many others, Charles Taylor, the author of a major study of secularization, has drawn attention to the fact that 'something has happened in the last half-century, perhaps even less, which has profoundly altered the conditions of belief in our societies'.[13] This shift he captures in his designation of the period through which we are now living as the 'Age of Authenticity'. By this he means the general acceptance of the idea that the way to a satisfied and fulfilled life is through recognizing that each of us must find and live out our own understanding of what it is to be human, and that we must resist any attempt that may be made to lay some other model upon us. A model that was not freely chosen would be 'inauthentic'. These inauthentic ways of living may be suggested to us or imposed upon us from outside by a past generation, family, the wider community, a political ideology or a church. This understanding of life, emerging with the Romantics at the end of the eighteenth century, had been taken for granted by many if not most intellectuals and members of the cultural elite for at least the past one hundred years. What happened in the 1960s was that, beginning with the younger generation, it gradually came to be accepted by almost everyone. It can be summed up in words used first by Polonius to Laertes in *Hamlet*:

> This above all: to thine own self be true,
> And it must follow, as the night the day,
> Thou canst not then be false to any man.[14]

Of course, the meaning intended by Shakespeare is rather different. Polonius is telling his son not to act in ways that will damage his reputation; to be true to his best interests. But 'to thine own self be true' is now often invoked to mean act authentically, live your life in the way you freely choose and not in ways imposed by others. It is not surprising that one of the more popular songs played at funerals in the nation's crematoria from this time was Frank Sinatra singing 'I did it my way'. 'My way' is the only authentic way. Everything else is false and insincere. This is also why for some people the journey of exploration, the search for the authentic self, is as important as having a settled faith. It is certainly more commendable and worthwhile than holding to the unexamined faith of your family or community.

This shift in sensibility presents churches with quite a challenge. It requires a certain type of congregation in which the explorer is as welcome as the committed believer and continuous spiritual exploration is accorded a high priority.

The extent to which people feel this need for authenticity and exploration has slowly been understood by Christians, and none more so, perhaps surprisingly, than evangelicals. The Alpha courses are an example of both the way in which the Church gives the impression that Christianity is all about beliefs yet also the way contemporary people, especially the younger generations, need space to think through their own positions and come to their own understanding. Those who designed the course want to commend to those who attend a rather conservative form of Christian belief. However, they recognize that the project will fail unless it allows time for discussion and for people to reach their own conclusions – authenticity. The fervent hope is that when they come to the end of the course they will gladly accept the Christian beliefs that have been presented to them; but they will do so because they have made that decision for themselves. This is the hope; it does not always go according to plan.

In an interview in the *Church Times*, the writer Alex Preston – whose novel *The Revelations* is about religion and the younger generation – spoke about his experience of attending an Alpha course in just these terms. He writes about his generation 'looking for some form of faith, some way of believing'. But this could not be something passed down. He could not simply accept someone else's beliefs: 'there seems to me to be a need to climb the mountain in your own way'. But in the end Preston was failed by Alpha. He wanted to be able to 'explore' and thought the Alpha course would allow him to do this. He found the experience 'highly seductive': it was full of young, single people and sexually highly charged. But the theology on offer was too restrictive, with an over-literalistic view of the Bible and an unhelpful attitude towards sex. Above all, the end-point still had to be the acceptance of a pre-packaged theology, a set of beliefs. One could not hold unorthodox beliefs and remain comfortably a member of the congregation. Nor could one be accepted as someone whose exploration had not yet come to an end, or might never come to an end.

One further consequence of the refusal to accept something handed down is that people now sit very lightly to particular denominations. There is no such thing as brand loyalty. People move quite freely from church to church, denomination to denomination. But the reasons they move between denominations is not necessarily a matter of beliefs, or not principally a matter of beliefs. Indeed, there seems to be a widespread acceptance on the part of many Christians that most Christians hold a core of beliefs in common, and what divides is more to do with types of liturgy and forms of worship. The distinctive denominational legacy is increasingly seen as unimportant or secondary. The day before I wrote these words I was presiding at an Anglican Eucharist in a local church. The person offering the intercessions was raised a Roman Catholic, the organist had been a Methodist, the first two communicants were a former Baptist and a practising Roman Catholic . . . and so on. The practising Roman Catholic comes to his local Anglican church most Sundays because it is nearer than the Roman Catholic Church and the Eucharist looks like a Roman Catholic Mass: the liturgical form is almost identical, the priest wears vestments, people make the sign of the cross, and so on. He takes no notice of official Roman Catholic attitudes towards Anglican orders, and the fact that the Anglican vicar is a woman is something he believes is as it should be. In other words, people are no longer buying into the total denominational package but making up their own minds – some would say picking and mixing.

In 2012 I addressed a group of about one hundred Anglican lay people and asked how many had been brought up in the Church of England. About one-third of hands were raised. The other two-thirds had a background in every other major denomination and some had moved between several. But even more interesting was the way they responded to a question about what they would do if their local Anglican church closed. The majority were very clear that they would go to the nearest church that best reflected or catered for what they thought of as their personal spirituality, whatever the denomination. This is now becoming more and more common yet it may go relatively unnoticed. It is a very recent phenomenon. In the past, it has generally been evangelicals who have found it easy to move between denominations in search of fellow evangelicals. Now it seems a more general phenomenon. In part this is to be explained by the impulse to find an expression of Christian faith that is more authentically one's own. It is a form of popular ecumenism brought about by the combined influence of a more secular culture and the need within that to find an authentic faith.

Having said this, we need to note that the only part of the Church of England that is growing is the evangelical. Here, holding correct belief is of central importance because our very salvation depends upon it. 'Correct' belief is an evangelical version of Christianity. At the heart of this is an understanding of what God in Christ has done for us. Human beings deserve the punishment of death for their sins for, as St Paul wrote, the wages of sin is death. But Christ substituted himself for us, dying in our place – a sacrificial death. However, because he was sinless, God raised him from death and restored him to life, eternal life. Those who understand this and put their trust in Christ are enabled to participate in this life: 'For God so loved the world that he gave his only Son, that whoever believes in him should not perish but have eternal life' (John 3.16). It is this doctrine that lies behind not only the experience of conversion but also the subsequent life of the Christian.

But 'correct' belief also extends to certain moral positions. In many ways, the ethical has become as important as the theological in recent years. It includes a rejection of same-sex sexual relationships, gay marriage and the ordination of homosexuals. It was liberal ethics rather than liberal theology that principally threatened the unity of the Anglican Communion throughout the period that Dr Rowan Williams was Archbishop of Canterbury (2003–12).

Faith and belief

The modern emphasis on beliefs can distract us from the real heart of Christian discipleship, which is faith. In the Gospels, Jesus often commends people for their faith or urges them to have faith. 'Faith' in this context is a matter of trust – in himself or in God, though perhaps we should say that the trust in him is trust in the One in whose name he speaks and acts. Whereas John the Baptist preached repentance, Jesus also urged faith:

> Have faith in God. Truly, I say to you, whoever says to this mountain, 'Be taken up and cast into the sea,' and does not doubt in his heart, but believes that what he says will come to pass, it will be done for him. (Mark 11.22–23)

Of course, if we press the matter and ask who this God is in whom we are to trust or have faith, we begin to set out beliefs. This is the God who made all that is, seen and unseen, who is loving and generous and faithful, whom Jesus calls Abba, Father. Behind or implicit in the act of faith are beliefs; but for the believer, the heart of the matter is trust in God, as we trust those we love, rather than some intellectual assent to a set of propositions. Even when Jesus urges his disciples to believe, he is speaking about trust. 'Let not your hearts be troubled; believe in God, believe also in me' (John 14.1).

Having faith does involve the intellect; we need to tell ourselves if not others that our faith is not irrational. But the emotions and the will are fully engaged as well. In theory, we might assent to Christian beliefs, yet be unable to commit in faith. But committing in faith is what opens a person to new possibilities. This is not easy. We might recall the occasion when the rich young man came to Jesus. He is a good person and convinced about the mission of Jesus. But Jesus, recognizing that something stands in the way of a full-hearted response, tells him to forgo his wealth. The young man goes away sorrowing 'for he had many possessions'. He cannot give up his dependence on material things.

But Jesus came to a religious culture in which the presence of God was taken for granted. This is not our situation now, though there may be some contemporary Christians whose faith is not often troubled and who may, therefore, take the beliefs implicit in faith for granted.

Faith and doubt

Faith is sometimes contrasted with doubt, not least by those who are very vocal and very noisy evangelists, anxious that people believe certain propositions – about the Bible, God and Jesus – and believe them with all their heart and mind, casting out all doubt. But the opposite of faith is not doubt but certainty. If we know something to be true beyond the possibility of contradiction – certainty – then we do not need faith. This is the point of the dialogue in John's Gospel between the Risen Jesus and 'doubting' Thomas. In this respect, Thomas is a very modern type of believer: unless he can see for himself he will not believe. The evangelist records the doubt of Thomas because he knows that many will come after who will never have the certainty of sight that he did and yet will believe. The Risen Lord calls them 'blessed' (John 20.29).

Certainty is scarcely possible in most areas of life: at best we can talk about the balance of probabilities or a high chance or significant correlation; but we can rarely say something is true beyond any chance of it being refuted. This is the case in human relationships: however much husband or wife think they know one another, they can never be certain beyond peradventure that the other does not harbour some secret; their relationship is built on trust not certainty. It is true in science: however secure a theory may seem, however convincing the evidence may be, every scientific hypothesis is in principle open to refutation. Why, then, should things be different when it comes to religion?

We can see why believers may think that religion is different. If we say that Christian believing is more like trusting in another person than accepting as true a set of propositions, what we do not want to do is seem to imply that God might turn out to be untrustworthy, in the way that sometimes a married person discovers the partner they put their faith in has been lying or cheating. There are several things we can say about this.

First, God may not change but our knowledge and understanding of God needs to be able to change. With time, experience and new knowledge, believers need to be able to refine and adjust their understanding, otherwise they may find themselves entertaining or defending an understanding of God that can no longer be held in all conscience. We should not fear this. On the contrary we should note a similar journey of discovery that Jesus makes. The Gospel of Luke is especially illuminating. In one of the infancy narratives we are told that Jesus 'grew in wisdom' as well as stature. At the age of 12 we find him in the Temple asking questions, presumably because he did not know the answers. In the wilderness his faith is not only tested but shaped by his struggle and reflection. In the Garden of Gethsemane he is still learning and understanding further the will of the Father as he prays for the cup to be taken from him. On the cross he wonders whether he has misunderstood after all: 'My God, my God, why hast thou forsaken me?' (Psalm 22.1). This cry may be even more significant than it first appears. In one breath Jesus may be pouring out his doubt and despair while at the same time committing himself in faith to the Father since the rest of the psalm recalls God's faithfulness towards both the people of Israel and the psalmist. One of the things that life may teach us is that even as faith is tested to breaking point we may yet find consolation in it.

Second, when the Church feels under pressure or threatened it is always tempted to claim more than it can or should. It fears having to say God remains a mystery or that we can say so much and no more. This seems weak in the face of aggressive criticism and attack. But as a result it over-claims. This is why some Christians may be nervous about too much theology and doctrinal certainty. It seems odd to say we live by faith – which always allows for doubt – yet we can make definitive doctrinal statements, and with such certainty that at times we have been prepared to put to death anyone who denied what the Church proclaimed. Yet in the first centuries the Church knew very well that there ought to be some caution in making claims about God. This was the starting point for an entire theological approach – *apophatic* or negative theology – that insisted that while we could say what was not true of God, we had to be cautious about making positive statements. This was an attempt to preserve the mystery of God and to remind human beings that we can never hope to capture in words and propositions the whole truth about God. Gregory of Nazianzus (329/30–389/90), one of the Cappadocian Fathers, wrote this:

> But to comprehend the whole of so great a Subject as this is quite impossible and impracticable, not merely to the utterly careless and ignorant, but even to those who are highly exalted, and who love God, and in like manner to every created nature; seeing that the darkness of this world and the thick covering of the flesh is an obstacle to the full understanding of the truth . . . For it is one thing to be persuaded of the existence of a thing, and quite another to know what it is.[15]

The spirit of this approach can be seen in some of the hymns we sing that have their origins in these early centuries, such as:

> Let all mortal flesh keep silence,
> and with fear and trembling stand;
> ponder nothing earthly minded,
> for with blessing in his hand
> Christ our God on earth descendeth,
> our full homage to demand.

The same theme is picked up in this nineteenth-century hymn:

> Immortal, invisible, God only wise,
> in light inaccessible hid from our eyes,
> most blessed, most glorious, the Ancient of Days,
> almighty, victorious, thy great name we praise . . .
>
> Great Father of glory, pure Father of light,
> thine angels adore thee, all veiling their sight;
> all laud we would render: O help us to see
> 'tis only the splendour of light hideth thee.

In more recent times, the Swiss Protestant theologian Karl Barth (1886–1968) took this apophatic stance as the starting point for his theology. Barth argued that the human reason could not by its own power attain to a knowledge of God. He called all attempts to do so 'religion' – a pejorative word for him. Knowledge of God had to come from God's side, from his choosing to reveal himself, which he did in Jesus Christ. Similarly, the French philosopher Simone Weil (1909–43), a Jew who was attracted to Christianity and who was concerned all her life with what it was possible to know, insisted that it was not possible for the human mind to grasp the full reality of God. What the mind did grasp could not be God. We could, therefore, deceive ourselves very badly if we thought that reality consisted of what little we were able to take hold of. Reaching out beyond what was graspable to God was a matter of faith. She called this 'negative faith'.

In many ways, all that these theologians and philosophers are doing is reminding us of the second of the Ten Commandments: that we should beware of making images of God: 'You shall not make for yourself a graven image, or any likeness of anything that is in heaven above, or that is in the earth beneath, or that is in the water under the earth.'[16] We can just as easily create an idol with words as with wood or stone.

The demand for certainty and the apparent offer of certainty by some Christians has seriously distorted the Christian witness and mission in a secular, scientific and plural age. It allows little or even no room for insights from other religions, it makes exploration suspect and it becomes difficult for those who have faith yet struggle with belief – an inevitable condition in which many will find themselves in a culture where religious belief is under such great pressure. Above all, the demand for both certainty and intimacy at all times inures against the sense of God's mysterious presence, which sometimes presses upon us and sometimes seems far from us.

One person who has written about this is the former poet laureate, Andrew Motion. He wrote in 2010 about his spiritual journey. His childhood included considerable exposure to the Church of England and its liturgies. His family were churchgoers in a village on the Suffolk–Essex border where 'the church played a time-honoured role in local life'. His father was a churchwarden and treasurer. He was sent to the church primary school and then to an Anglo-Catholic secondary school. He became a conventional believer, sometimes quite zealous. Then when he was 17 his mother had a serious accident and he began to question much that he had come to believe. He could no longer see any connection between a person's character and their lot in life.[17] He came to think that at best the world was random and God a delusion. At worst 'it was a kind of celestial North Korea' – a phrase he borrows from Christopher Hitchens. Although he occasionally had 'spurts of orthodox feeling', he stayed in this atheistic state for the next 30 years. Then he met a priest whose sermons he admired and found thought-provoking. It reconnected him with his past. 'Specifically,' he wrote, 'he matched my much sharper sense of mortality with the feeling of settledness and connection I had known as a child.' Now he feels moved by memories, music, the language of the Prayer Book and the King James Bible, and opened up to be more receptive. This is not conventional faith but something more ambiguous, a faith that 'flickers on and off like a badly wired lamp' or where 'honest doubt comes and goes, and in doing so keeps alive the argument with and about God'.

The persistence of belief

What strikes me about the present age is the persistence of belief among the general population in such secular times. One example will suffice. In March 2012, during a football match at White Hart Lane, one of the players, Fabrice Muamba, collapsed. The crowd fell silent as it gradually became clear that something was seriously wrong. The player lay prostrate on the pitch and the crowd looked on as doctors desperately tried to keep his heart beating. Eventually the game was abandoned and Muamba taken to hospital. Within minutes of the incident happening people began to pray for the stricken player both in the ground and beyond. On the field, Rafael van der Vaart fell to his knees and people realized that he was praying. Many in the crowd followed and within a very short time the social networks were urging people to 'Pray4Muamba'. For several days messages were posted by fans and footballers alike saying that they were praying for Muamba: 'Come on Fabrice Muamba, praying for you', tweeted Rio Ferdinand; and similar sentiments were expressed by Wayne Rooney and Stuart Holden. Soon 'Pray4Muamba' was appearing on T-shirts. Owen Coyle, the manager of Muamba's club, Bolton Wanderers, a Christian, noted that 'Prayer was the most used word of the weekend'. Muamba survived, though his heart had stopped for some 78 minutes and the cardiac specialist who treated him in the ground and at the London Chest Hospital called it 'miraculous'.[18]

This impressive and widespread response to the near-death of a footballer was noted by journalists with some astonishment. *The Guardian's* sports writer, Richard Williams, describing himself as 'one who veers between a vague agnosticism and, in darker moods, outright atheism', devoted an entire column to trying to make sense of it all. At any period until relatively recently, it would have required no comment. But Williams felt impelled to remark on a phenomenon that he would not have anticipated. He dismissed the idea that this was simply something self-indulgent and exaggerated. It was not like the mass outpourings of grief following the death of Princess Diana. This was 'genuine sorrow' and it was 'spontaneous and authentic'.[19] (How he knew this was not revealed to us.) He mused on whether people were really praying 'in the conventional sense' or only saying they were, though that only begs the question as to why praying was deemed to be an appropriate thing to ask people to do and why so many seemed to be doing it. Was it just 'superstitious ritual' and 'a means of comforting ourselves'? However, why superstitious rituals should comfort was not explained. 'Can agnostics and atheists pray too?' he wondered. In the end, he left the last word in his article to the vicar of Bolton, a football fan, who remarked that at some point in our lives 'all people pray' and seek to 'connect with the transcendent, however we conceive it' and that this provides a means of expressing 'that well of compassion we've all got within us'.

What I found of interest in this whole episode was the fact that after over two decades of sustained attack on religion, its beliefs and practices, here were large numbers of people – thousands if not millions of football fans across the country – who were urging prayer and praying for a young man, a refugee to this country, so cruelly struck down. It is, of course, impossible to know how many prayed; but whatever the numbers, many did pray, and if we were to press them I have no doubt that their prayers were offered in what Richard Williams called the conventional sense, by which I guess he meant that they prayed to a loving God.

In any assessment of religious belief in Britain today this ought to be as significant a piece of evidence as the information gathered from opinion polling. There is what people say. There is what people do. The prayers for Fabrice Muamba were offered by football supporters across the country just a month or two after a YouGov poll found that 76 per cent of people were 'not religious'. This figure must have included some of those same fans who within a few weeks found themselves praying.[20]

Becoming a believer

Often, what draws people to church is the realization that as we make our way through life we are compelled to acknowledge sooner or later that our flourishing and fulfilment depend on making our own, as far as possible, a range of values that did not originate with us. Love, compassion, mercy, truth, justice, fidelity are a core of key virtues that are recognized by both the world's great religions and the secular cultures that have emerged from them. As Kant once noted, we feel the force of them and they command our allegiance. We know that if we try to live without them or oppose them, in the end this will be self-defeating. It will not lead to our flourishing but rather issue in misery and frustration. In addition, there are also times when we feel the mysterious presence of something, someone, beyond ourselves.

How are we to understand these kinds of experience that many people are aware of and in more reflective moments will speak about? One way of making sense of them is to recognize that they are quite compatible with religion and the Christian faith.[21] But we need moments when we can reflect on these things, and churches are one place where we can do this. But if churches are not going to be there in the future, or churches become places that more and more people feel are alien places rather than welcoming, what then?

In the first century, when St Paul began to take the gospel to Gentiles as well as Jews, he said this to the men of Athens on the Areopagus: 'Men of Athens . . . as I passed along, and observed the objects of your worship, I found also an altar with this inscription, "To an unknown god." What therefore you worship as unknown, this I proclaim to you' (Acts 17.22–23). But suppose Paul were to return. How would he commend the Christian faith to the men and women of contemporary Athens, many of whom, like other Europeans, are possibly somewhere between belief and unbelief. He might want to begin like this:

> We can't simply decide to become a believer by some act of will. But life can nudge us towards a belief in God if we act in ways that don't close down the possibility. If we come to church week by week and open ourselves to the liturgy, to sacred music, to the Scriptures and to those we meet there, we may well find that we do have faith even if, like a badly wired lamp, it flickers on and off.

Brian Mountford, who is vicar of St Mary the Virgin, the University Church in Oxford, published in 2010 the results of conversations he had had with 12 members of his congregation who were not believers. One of them, however, Mary Zacaroli, indicated how she thought her non-belief might grow into faith. She said this:

> I come to this church because you're not trying to grab my soul. I can bring my jumbled thoughts and just live with them, knowing that no one will try to convert me. You see, it's the ritual of going to church that's important for me – something to hang on to. I feel I need that especially when my life is anarchic and chaotic, and I hope that, maybe, by practising the ritual I'll find my faith growing.[22]

Mary also has hopes for her children. She wants to be able to give them a Christian upbringing so that they share her 'moral compass'.

Conclusion

What all of this suggests is that we cannot assume – perhaps we never could – that in today's congregations there is homogeneity of belief. It is going to be a mixed picture. I would summarize what I have found over the years in this way:

- There are those who believe 'firmly and truly' in traditional formulations of Christian doctrine.
- There are others who spend little time examining Christian beliefs. They take a few basic doctrines for granted because for them the heart of the matter is not a set of beliefs but personal experience of the mystery we call God. This awareness of God's presence may be at particular moments, such as during prayer or when reading the Bible or receiving the sacrament; they may also include times in the countryside or working with the homeless. They would agree with St Francis of Assisi, who told his brothers to go and preach the gospel using words if necessary.
- Many are prepared to be quite tentative in their believing and to recognize that they also entertain many doubts and uncertainties. They welcome a Church that is not dogmatic and not afraid of debate.
- Some prefer to speak as little as possible about the mystery that is God.
- There are some who do not believe in any conventional sense at all, but are not unduly anxious about this.

Historically, the Church of England has been a Church where people of deep faith, honest doubters and struggling believers could find a home – a broad Church in this sense too. But all the debate and discussion in the contemporary Church of England is not about how this welcome can be extended further but about ensuring that the Church becomes a place of 'correct' belief, in faith and morals. It is becoming harder for some people to feel comfortable in a growing number of churches.

I suspect that there are many people in the contemporary West who would find that what Andrew Motion writes about resonates with their own experience. Some would say they were not religious. Others, like Motion, would say they were not conventionally religious. But the line between them is not always clear. Open agnosticism and forms of belief overlap and shade into one another and make it very hard to believe that the West is quite as secular as some secularists would have us believe.

At any rate, what we can say is that, for all of us, believing is always going to be a work in progress. In the past, the Church of England always knew that.

4

Reclaiming Lost Church

———•◆•———

I don't believe in God, but I miss him.
>   *Julian Barnes, in* Nothing to be Frightened of

Religions understand that to belong to a community is both very desirable and not very easy.
>   *Alain de Botton, atheist, philosopher and writer*

I have suggested throughout these chapters that we have created problems for ourselves by trying to think about the relationship of the British to the Church and Christianity, especially the Church of England, by using two categories – attending and believing – when we really needed three: attending, believing and belonging. I have looked at how attending and believing have changed in the period since the Second World War. But my main focus has been on those who belong to the Church of England yet who are too easily overlooked whenever religion and society are discussed. The Lost Church of the title is the Church that once guaranteed a home for those who knew they belonged even if they were not great attenders and struggled to believe. However, in more recent times a growing number of people who once felt they belonged do so no more.

In this final chapter, therefore, I want to ask why it should be that many people now find the Church of England an alien and not a welcoming place. I want to suggest that at some point in the last few years a sizeable number of regularly practising Anglicans began to understand the role of the Church of England differently and that this is an accelerating trend. For them, the traditional model of the Church of England plays little or no part in their understanding or practice. They may even have consciously rejected it. It has led to the growth of a sectarian temper. This in turn leads those who in the past had a sense of belonging to feel uneasy and unsure. The book as a whole is a plea for lay and ordained alike to stop and take stock before the broad and inclusive Church that the Church of England always was and that finds its expression in the idea of the parish church, is lost beyond recall. If we are serious about ministering to the people of England and not just preaching at them, this is a mission and ministry that needs serious attention by laity and clergy alike.

How the Church was lost

Sometimes people have been alienated and the Church lost to them as a consequence of something very deliberately and consciously done by the Church. At other times the alienation has been an unintended consequence of decisions. Overall, it is hard to know whether the transformation of the Church into a less welcoming organization is intended or accidental. Either way, it is happening. The company of 'belongers' is thinning out.

Intended consequences

We have already outlined in previous chapters some of the ways in which the Church of England over the past few decades has intentionally made it more difficult for those who are not regular attenders to continue to feel that they belong. Some of this has been the result of decisions taken at a national, diocesan or local level that reflect a changing understanding of the Church. This has shown itself most obviously in attitudes towards the pastoral offices. As we saw in the first chapter, it became more difficult for people to have their child baptized if they were not regular churchgoers, or to get married if they had been married previously. In some parishes, infant baptism is no longer offered at all, and some clergy will neither marry divorcees themselves nor allow other clergy to do so in the church where they are the incumbent. Changes in attitude towards baptism reflected a view that the boundary between churchgoers and others must be made more hard-edged. It was thought that the way to turn casual and irregular attendance into greater commitment was to put an end to the idea that people had some sort of entitlement to the baptism of a child, as if the Church of England were the spiritual arm of the National Health Service. Although attitudes towards divorce changed over this time, the memory of being rebuffed hardened the hearts of many against the Church. The same happened with those families that were refused baptism for their children. All added to the impression that the less regular attender was no longer welcome. Something similar is happening with that small minority who want the Church to bless their civil partnership but have been turned away. The point about memories is that individuals do not keep them to themselves but they are rehearsed within families and communities and play a part in shaping attitudes more widely and down the generations.

From time to time the Church put on an unwelcoming face for other reasons of principle. Some of these could be quite bizarre. As a student in Cambridge in the late 1960s, I recall Professor Geoffrey Lampe recounting an occasion when he was once on holiday. He was bicycling through East Anglia looking for somewhere to receive Holy Communion on the following Sunday. He eventually saw a church situated somewhat inconveniently at a great distance from the road. After struggling across fields and up a hill he finally reached the building. On the door was a notice: 'Communicants of the Church of South India are not welcome here.' This was an echo of a dispute about the validity of orders in a Church created from a number of Protestant denominations, including Anglicans, in India; some Anglo-Catholics took exception to this ecumenical Church because not all of its clergy were episcopally ordained. But what would the casual visitor conclude from finding such a notice? Similar internal disputes have turned others away. Women students have often given me accounts over the years of sermons they have had to sit through that have decried the ordination of women in terms that would have been quite unacceptable in other contexts and ought not to have been tolerated in the Church. Preachers seemed quite unaware of the impact their words were having on some in their congregation. I remember going to support former students of mine who were among the first women ever to be ordained in their diocese, and who had been waiting many years for the possibility. The diocesan bishop, an opponent of women's ordination, took no part in their being made deacon, yet nevertheless felt it appropriate to preach. He failed to mention at any point in his sermon the historic significance of what was happening.

The points of principle today are often less to do with matters of church order or the pastoral offices and more to do with questions of morality and belief. We are becoming less tolerant and less generous in our approach as we become more anxious about growth and the Church's place in a multi-faith society. We are repeatedly told that churches only grow if there is a real cost to belonging: the Church of England must be much clearer about what is correct belief and what is not, what is the right moral position and what is not, who is a Christian and who is not, who is in and who is out. Congregations of this sort are becoming more prevalent and they are indeed more likely to be growing. They tend to be evangelical, though not all evangelical churches are of this kind. Overall, evangelical churches represented about 40 per cent of the Church of England in 2012, an increase from 26 per cent in 1969.[1] This is the direction of travel that the Church is taking and it is from these churches that increasing numbers of ordinands will come. It means that within a few years many, perhaps the majority of Church of England parishes will be staffed by clergy from an evangelical background, even if this does not represent the current theological position of the parish. Many of these ordinands and clergy will have little or no first-hand experience of any other part of the Church of England and may have received little explicit teaching during training about the historic role of the Church of England and its ecclesiology, for which they may have, in any case, little sympathy.

Unintended consequences

But the changing nature of the local church can also be the result of unintended consequences. Let me take an example. In 2009 an English diocesan synod adopted this as what it called its 'vision statement':

> The Diocese of . . . is called to grow a sustainable network of Christ-like, lively and diverse Christian communities in every place which are effective in making disciples and seeking to transform our society and God's world.

At first glance, few Christians might want to quarrel with that. Indeed, when I asked a group of men and women training for ordained ministry in the diocese what they made of the statement, they were all enthusiastic about it. However, when I asked them to explain what the vision statement meant, the more they said the more they divided. One group interpreted it to mean that the diocese was going to put more effort into supporting the existing 'network' of parish churches so that each congregation might become more lively, attract more worshippers and be outward in its focus. The other group read the statement to mean that the diocese was not committed to supporting existing churches at all but rather intended to create alongside them new congregations meeting elsewhere in the parish. This group explained that too many churches were hopelessly moribund and beyond saving. They had to die in order that lively, alternative congregations could flourish in their place. Resurrection, they explained, only came after prior death. These new congregations might be church plants or 'fresh expressions of Church'. They might meet in an existing church, at a different time from the present, poorly attended services, or, more likely, they would meet in some other building. Either way, they would not be related or accountable to the churches in whose parishes they were established. In their account there was no mention of the parish because their imagination was not informed by that model. The Church for them was not organized parochially but consisted of gathered congregations of like-minded people seeking out souls to add to their number. Where they met and the buildings they met in were of secondary consideration.

When the first group heard what the second group said, they were perplexed. Was the vision statement ambiguous or had they misunderstood? If they had misunderstood, had there been others at the synod who also misunderstood and who had, as a consequence, voted for something whose implications were not fully appreciated by them? Perhaps the intention was to allow churches to establish in their own parishes alternative congregations to meet the needs of particular groups of people. If this was the intention, could it be exploited by those who really have no time for Church of England congregations that are different from themselves; parish churches that fail the test of correct beliefs?

A careful reading of the statement does not really allow for ambiguity, but that is not the same as saying that those who voted for it fully realized what some of the consequences might be. This is a diocese that has now committed itself to creating a series of alternative congregations to the existing parish churches – a kind of parallel Church. This is exactly what has been happening since the resolution was passed. New congregations have been created, sometimes – where a church has welcomed them – meeting at a separate time from an existing congregation, sometimes meeting elsewhere. Most have been 'church plants' from existing parish churches or other non-parochial congregations. The bishop has sometimes been 'informed' that a plant is going to happen, sometimes not. The local clergy have generally discovered indirectly. The church plants in this diocese do not relate to any of the local Church of England structures – parish, deanery or even diocese – but go their own way, making whatever alliances they choose, usually with similar, sympathetic groups, not necessarily Anglican. At least one plant – though not the parish church from which it sprang – regards itself as in communion with an African archbishop rather than the diocesan bishop or the Archbishop of Canterbury. In reality they are accountable to no one – except the Holy Spirit – even though the question of accountability is an issue to which they often refer. Some of them are among the largest congregations in the diocese. I doubt whether more than a minority of synod understood the outcome of the statement to which they put their names in 2009, yet it is that statement that has encouraged those planting congregations to do so without necessarily informing let alone obtaining the goodwill of the parish clergy in whose parishes they appear. One such planted congregation quite explicitly calls itself 'Anglican' yet has no sense that Anglicanism in England takes the form of the Church of England! At the time of writing it is seeking to meet in a community centre that is a few yards away from the parish church with whom, for the moment, it has had no contact. (It would find any contact an uncomfortable experience since it rejects the leadership of women in the Church, but the vicar, readers and churchwardens of the parish church are all female.)

All of this raises many questions for the Church of England. One is the important matter of sustainability. The history of Christianity is one of revivals and new movements that, where there is no institutional base, rise and fall and disappear, leaving behind former worshippers bruised and bereft. I was a parish priest in Sheffield in 1986 when the Nine O'Clock Services (an emanation of St Thomas Crookes) began to sweep up younger people from my parish – which was near to St Thomas – and across the city for their technologically sophisticated acts of worship. Young adults came in hundreds and eventually had to move into a complex in the town centre for their meetings. Although nominally Anglican, they played no part in Church of England structures and rather despised what they saw as the Laodicean hopelessness of existing parish churches. But congregations that are accountable to no one, and only have time for those Christians who look like themselves, are always in danger of producing leaders who become hubristic. Leadership in such congregations may do wonders for the ego but it can be fatal for the soul. The Nine O'Clock Service congregation began to resemble a cult, with an unhealthy dependency on a small leadership group, one of whom was fast-tracked to ordination by the archdeacon and bishop. The Christian ideals of the young people were eventually betrayed by the leader and the whole experiment collapsed amid allegations of sexual and emotional abuse. But not before many people were damaged and hurt. The 'fresh expression' – the term had not then been coined – collapsed and disappeared. The despised parish churches endured – but they might not in the future if they are seriously and systematically undermined.

I have no way of knowing how many similar congregations exist elsewhere in the country, and perhaps the Nine O'Clock Service was an extreme example and one from which lessons have been learnt. From what I observe, however, the importance of accountability is acknowledged in theory but not translated into anything meaningful in practice – being part of the deanery structure would, for example, be a minimum requirement. But however many such congregations there are, it points to a phenomenon that the national Church should be anxious about. There ought to be concern whenever congregations are created outside existing structures, without clear lines of accountability and in opposition to the Church of England model of the Church. One feature of some of the new plants and fresh expressions is their contempt for the parochially based model of the Church with its commitment to a ministry towards those who belong but neither attend regularly nor believe in the way these leaders prescribe. It is this – the growth within the Church of a sectarian temper – that is a real and growing threat to the future of the Church of England.

Four characteristics of the Church of England

What, then, is the understanding of the Church that the Church of England has stood for since its beginning and that is now threatened? Let me comment on four particular aspects.

Protestant

First, the Church of England is 'Protestant'. But there is a particular flavour to its Protestantism. The Reformation in England was not simply a matter of reproducing an English version of the Catholic Church. Even though the first reforms were relatively conservative, the Elizabethan Settlement was an attempt to create a national Church that could embrace as wide a spectrum of belief as possible. It was not about establishing an alternative central authority and a single version of Christian faith. The Church believed that this was both undesirable and unachievable. The institutional Church makes it clear in one of its foundation documents – the Thirty-Nine Articles of Faith in the Book of Common Prayer – that no Church or Council of the Church can claim for itself infallibility in matters of doctrine. Any Church that thinks it has the right to make such a claim and act upon it sets off on a journey that sooner or later leads to some form of repression or tyranny, as Christian history shows only too easily.

All Christian Churches – the pre-Reformation Catholic Church, the post-Reformation Protestant and Roman Catholic Churches – have attempted at different times and in different ways to root out expressions of Christianity with which they disagreed. In Europe, the great religious upheaval that we call the Reformation was preceded by numerous minor struggles and persecutions. At various times, heretics and the theologically unorthodox were imprisoned, tortured, commanded to keep silent or killed. In England, the scholar John Wycliffe (1328–84) was put to death for his dissenting views on such matters as eucharistic teaching and the translation of the Bible into the vernacular. Those who agreed with him, the Lollards, were persecuted. The Czech priest Jan Huss (1369–1415) was burnt at the stake for unorthodox opinions and a wish to reform the Church. After his death five papal crusades were directed against his followers. During the Reformation, Protestants of one type killed Protestants of another. Calvinists in Geneva drowned Anabaptists in the Lake because they would not accept infant baptism. After the Reformation, Protestants and Roman Catholics plunged Europe into decades of conflict and wars that only ended with the Peace of Westphalia in 1648, as a result of which states became either Catholic or Protestant according to the convictions of their rulers. But while the Peace of Westphalia marked the end of religious wars it did not end attempts by Churches to maintain control over beliefs and suppress alternatives.

The principal instruments of the Catholic Church for dealing with heresies were the Inquisitions, culminating in the establishment of the Congregation of the Holy Office of the Inquisition at the Vatican in 1542. Persecution was sometimes successful, sometimes not. The Cathars of southern France and the Waldensians of northern Italy were harassed over three centuries. The Cathars were finally eliminated in France by the early 1300s. However, Waldensian churches continue in Italy and the United States to this day. Nor did the Church confine its interest to religious matters alone. There was a long, though ultimately unsuccessful, struggle against the emergence of modern astronomy. The views of Galileo Galilei (1564–1642) – that the earth rotated around the sun and not vice versa – in the end could not be suppressed even though he was made to recant them and held under house arrest.

As the nineteenth century progressed, it became increasingly apparent that the ability of the Church in Europe to exercise any direct control over people's belief and behaviour was draining away. The modern secular state promoted the right of individuals to hold and express their own ideas. It also began to erode the ability of the Church to influence the next generation through its monopoly of the education system. By and large, Protestants either accepted or welcomed these developments, seeing them as inevitable in democracies. The Roman Catholic Church responded differently, seeking to reassert the spiritual authority of the papacy in matters of faith and morals with the formal declaration of papal infallibility in 1870. Thereafter, particular popes used their authority to silence any of whose teaching they disapproved, such as the Swiss theologian Hans Küng (1928–), the nun and academic Sister Margaret Farley and the liberation theologian Leonardo Boff (1938–). Küng was prevented from teaching Catholic theology at the University of Tübingen, though he remained a priest 'in good standing' and continued to teach 'ecumenical theology'. Farley's liberal stance on Christian sexual ethics in her book, *Just Love: A Framework for Christian Sexual Ethics*, was condemned by the Vatican in 2012. Boff was treated more severely. In 1985 he was silenced for a year by the Holy Office, which was then directed by Cardinal Joseph Ratzinger, now Pope Benedict XVI. The Church took exception to his book, *Church: Charism and Power*, accusing Boff of politicizing the gospel. Boff called this 'religious terrorism'. He eventually left the Franciscan order and his priestly ministry.

The doctrine of papal infallibility has had two quite different and opposite consequences in the modern Roman Catholic Church. On the one hand, it paradoxically led to an undermining of the influence of the *magisterium* in some sections of the Church, most notably in parts of Europe and North America, where Roman Catholicism existed alongside equally numerous or more numerous Protestant denominations. Many Roman Catholic faithful found themselves rejecting the official teaching of the Church on some ethical matters, notably contraception and divorce. It was soon obvious that middle-class Roman Catholic families in, say, Germany or the United States were producing no more children than their Protestant counterparts. On the whole, Roman Catholics here seemed happy to be Catholics on Sunday but Protestant the rest of the week. The authority of the Pope was weakened. But in Ireland, until relatively recently, the picture was very different. The infallibility of the Pope was not only accepted in theory but decisively influenced the attitude of ordinary Catholics towards the Church and its (male) clergy in practice. This produced in Ireland – and other countries where the Roman Catholic presence was strong – a general church ethos that Protestants have found objectionable since the first days of the Reformation. This is a culture in which clergy are deferred to and put beyond criticism. We have seen the very dark side of this in the child abuse scandals that have been rocking the Church since the early 1990s. Abusing clergy were not reported to the appropriate authorities or the police by their superiors but simply moved to another appointment. Even when incidents came to light there developed a pattern of cover-up. In Ireland in particular it was clear that the laity and the authorities were also just as likely to turn a blind eye, excuse or cover up. There were even accusations that Pope Benedict had impeded the work of investigation when as Prefect of the Congregation for the Doctrine of the Faith he wrote to bishops in 2001 reminding them that details of allegations of sexual abuse against minors should not be made public and were reserved to the jurisdiction of the Congregation. Many of those who were abused as children have now told their stories, explaining how they were victimized. Both men and women said they believed they had to submit to the will of God as that had been mediated through the priesthood.

Women often added to this by saying that what was happening to them could not be questioned but simply had to be borne, like Mary: 'Be it unto me according to your word' (Luke 1.38). They have spoken too of the way their lives have subsequently been blighted – the problems they had in later years with sex or in forming intimate relationships. They talked about the difficulties they had in being left alone in a room with one other person. Some said they could never trust priests again, or the Church, or God. These are the baleful consequences that flow from an organization that makes claims to absolute authority and expects its followers to show suitable deference and to obey.

Protestants have no such central authority, though attempts by particular churches, or groups of Christians within particular denominations, to assert what they considered the 'fundamentals' of Christianity was a parallel development. Evangelicalism has been especially prone to this tendency.

The history of theological repression, and the culture produced by an authoritarian institution, ought to serve as a warning to contemporary Anglicans who may be tempted to claim for themselves the kind of authority the Articles caution against. However, this is not how some in the Church of England now see matters: they do want to be more prescriptive about faith and morals because they believe this will lead to church growth. It seems that the lessons of history, and the more contemporary lessons of the Nine O'Clock Service, have still not been learnt. Perhaps they never are. There will always be those who believe they are beyond the possibility of such corruption – because they are under the direct influence of God's Holy Spirit. This is why the Protestantism of the Church of England should be understood not in terms of some specific set of beliefs – a Westminster Confession, for example – but in terms of the Articles, especially Article XXI, that the councils of the Church 'may err, and sometimes have erred, even in things pertaining unto God'. The Church of England's Protestantism is one that rejects central authority and recognizes that there will always be some matters of faith and morality on which not all Christians will see eye to eye.

One important corollary of this is that attempts by some catholic Anglicans to seek reconciliation with the Roman Catholic Church are always going to fail since the way the Roman Catholic Church understands authority runs counter to the Church of England's basic understanding. The idea that the Roman Catholic Church might one day accept that another Church that does not share its own understanding of authority can nevertheless be part of some greater Catholic Church is pure illusion. This remains the fundamental stumbling block to Christian unity and marks off all other Churches from the Roman Catholic Church. It is why those Anglican priests who broke away after 2009 to become part of the so-called personal Ordinariate had to be re-ordained. Their Anglican orders counted for nothing. They had to become Roman Catholic priests and any concessions that were made to their previous Anglican life were only that – concessions. They could be withdrawn at any moment.

The Church of England is first of all a Protestant Church, but it is a form of Protestantism that has not sought to be overly prescriptive. It does not believe in making windows into people's souls.

Inclusive

A second characteristic of the Church of England follows from the fact that from its inception it has tried to be the Church of all the people of England. It understood that if it were to be the Church of England, it would have to embrace within it a wide spectrum of theological opinion. It would have to be 'inclusive'. An inclusive or broad Church is what it was and is, and the range of views within it is often summarized as liberal, evangelical and catholic; this is how the Church describes Anglican opinion on its current website. In addition, the Church has gradually come to understand that pluralism extends beyond matters of theology. Human beings have different visions of the good life and what it is to live ethically. This is true for the human community in general but it is also true of the Christian community, albeit with much common ground. There is a world of difference between what the Amish congregations of the United States look for as the realization of God's kingdom on earth and what the average member of a Welsh Methodist church might envisage. There are different ideas about what constitutes appropriate behaviour as we await or prepare for the coming of that kingdom. But while we may have come to realize this, we are sometimes a long way from understanding or working out the implications of it.

Contemporary Anglicans in England seem less willing than they were to accept the idea that there can be theological and ethical pluralism. This may be because in times of existential uncertainty, when rapid change throws up bewilderingly new moral challenges, some people find it difficult to live with pluralism or provisionality; they yearn for definitive teaching in matters of faith and morals – as long as that teaching conforms with their own views. Sometimes the Church of England is criticized because it does not and cannot offer a set religious menu but seems to put before people something more à la carte. But this is the fundamental nature of the Church of England as an inclusive Church. If it were to demand that all lay and ordained Anglicans pass some test, other than what it has historically required, it will begin to depart quite seriously from what it fundamentally is. Yet more congregations are beginning to go down this path. We have seen that the growing parts of the Church put great emphasis on belief, or rather on particular beliefs – a particular theological approach and certain moral positions. There is less room in such churches for the less than orthodox, for those whose beliefs flicker on and off, or for those, still exploring, who can change their minds. These beliefs also extend to ethical matters. Indeed, it may be here that the insistence on 'correct belief' is even more pronounced. The ethical issue that has become something of a litmus test for 'sound belief' is that of homosexuality. All of this is alien to the spirit of Anglicanism.

It can have the effect of putting off those who might otherwise be prepared to give the Church a chance. Lucy Mangan, a columnist with *The Guardian*, is an example. In a weekend supplement she wrote about her experiences of taking her young child to a playgroup run by a church.[2] Mangan is a non-believer but hardly a militant atheist. She was quite content to have a prayer for the health of the babies at the end of the session and she acknowledges that she loved 'the language of the church and much else about it'. She also says that she is not a person who is easily stirred emotionally; her husband says she is 'technically a mineral'. Or so she thought. But on this occasion at the end of the session, the playgroup leader invited parents to sign a petition against gay marriage, explaining that it was for anyone who 'didn't believe in the destruction of family life' and who wanted 'little babies to grow up with a mother and father'. She lost her temper, objected to the petition on the grounds that this was an inappropriate time and place, and declared that this was a strange idea of Christian love. But what upset her almost more than the issue of gay marriage was what she called 'the sudden eruption of prejudice in our midst. The blind-siding. The glimpse of the unshakeable moral certainty that faith gives, which was apparent in [the playgroup leader's] assumption that her audience would share her views.'

She went on to say that the incident was 'useful' because it reminded her how 'rampant these sickening plagues still are, even if you've managed to banish them from your immediate circle of family and friends'. Her final comment about the church was the most telling of all: 'So, thank you playgroup lady. I was drawing closer. I shall keep a safer distance from now on.'

The playgroup lady has misunderstood both the nature of the Church of England as a broad Church and, equally seriously, the Church's approach to ethics. Anglican moral thinking – as exemplified, for instance, by the Litany – begins with the centrality of God as loving and generous, and the need for that to be reflected by Christians in their own practice. If they find themselves objecting to loving and generous behaviour on the grounds that it conflicts with some other principle, Anglicans need to pause and think carefully about how they are to resolve the apparent conflict. They would do well then to ponder the point made by Frederick Faber in his hymn, 'There's a wideness in God's mercy'. Faber, an Anglican priest who converted to Roman Catholicism, wrote this in the second verse:

> But we make his love too narrow
> by false limits of our own;
> and we magnify his strictness
> with a zeal he will not own.

In other words, Christians need to be clear about what it means to put love at the centre of Christian morality, especially in those instances where some other principle seems to contradict a generous action or a loving relationship – such as the repudiation of homosexuality on the basis of biblical texts. When this happens, we should be on our guard.

There have been many critical moments in Christian history when a seemingly secure moral position has had to be relinquished because it conflicted with the more important principle of love. The question of slavery is well understood. The practice went unquestioned by the Church for nearly two thousand years before it came to be seen as abhorrent to the mind of God: it denied the fundamental humanity of all those whose freedom was taken from them, and in their treatment violated the command to love one another.

It could be objected that slavery is not forbidden in the Scriptures whereas homosexuality is. This is true. The question is whether something forbidden in one social and historic context has a continuing validity. But again, there have been many instances where something that is forbidden in Scripture comes to be seen as not the will of God. Many of the practices noted in the book Leviticus, for instance, are no longer used as a guide to conduct because we now understand that no woman is a witch and menstruation does not 'pollute'. We might note the way John Calvin decided to overturn the biblical injunction against usury – lending money at interest. In effect he argued that there was a more important biblical principle that trumped it. For Calvin the issue was this: biblical texts about usury that were originally framed to stop the poor falling into debt-slavery were now preventing people from borrowing to finance enterprise. In a letter to a friend, he dealt with the matter in two ways. First, he considered the historic circumstances in which usury was banned. He concluded that the relevant texts made sense in their original context but not in the context of the sixteenth century: 'Our situation is quite different. For that reason I am unwilling to condemn it, as long as it is practised with equity and charity.' Indeed, to oppose a practice that would allow people to improve their material circumstances would be to 'play with God in a childish manner, preferring words over truth itself'. This leads to a second point. Calvin in effect invokes the idea of a hierarchy of moral values, as a result of which the more general principle of equity finds against the narrower matter of a continuing prohibition of usury. Calvin's overturning of what until then had seemed to be an absolute ban on usury resulted in the economic development of Europe and prosperity on a previously unimagined scale. Far from impoverishing people, usury could be the means of their enrichment.[3]

What we see in Calvin's argument in favour of usury is not a fuzzy liberal seeking to set aside a biblical injunction, but the recognition by a serious theologian that Christianity – and we could add any religion – needs a mechanism for allowing moral development. If it does not, then it condemns itself to moral irrelevancy as cultural circumstances shift. Calvin's bold assertion – 'Hence, I conclude that we ought not to judge usury according to a few passages of Scripture, but in accordance with the principle of equity' – freed people to engage in a thorough and much more constructive debate around the real issues of usury, not the matter of principle but the questions of practice. How do you safeguard the vulnerable from the predatory lender? What levels of interest are appropriate? What about the poor who are too poor even to borrow? Those same questions will always need to be asked, not least in our own day when so many are becoming impoverished as a result of reckless lending and borrowing.

Returning to the question of homosexual relationships, even if we thought there was a biblical principle that prohibited them, it is not at all obvious that it has to be preferred over other principles when they conflict. In this case the conflict is between that principle and human flourishing; the judgement is that a society in which homosexual people are able to have stable, loving relationships is more cohesive than one where such relationships are either forbidden or frowned upon. The hymn I quoted above goes on to say:

> For the love of God is broader
> than the scope of human mind,
> and the heart of the Eternal
> is most wonderfully kind.
> If our love were but more simple,
> we should take him at his word;
> and our hearts would find assurance
> in the promise of the Lord.

The mistake critics of the Church of England often make is to assume that in order to maintain the traditional Anglican role, the clergy have to be bland. This is not so. But there is a world of difference between having strong opinions and seeking to close down the opinions of others. The Church of England stands for an open and welcoming approach that recognizes that there will always be theological and ethical differences between us. It does not insist on holding 'correct' beliefs and moral positions. It can take both plurality in doctrine and provisionality in morality in its stride.

National

A third feature of the Church of England is that it is the national Church of the English people. It is not and never has been the Church of all the English people, but it is by law established, Parliament continues to legislate for its liturgies and the monarch is its Supreme Governor. There are two aspects to this that are important. First, the Church plays a role in national life, especially on major national occasions and at critical moments. Many of these are also associated with the Royal Family. The Church baptizes, marries, crowns and buries monarchs. It is responsible for annual services of remembrance at the Cenotaph and in the Albert Hall. It provides chaplains to the armed forces and the Houses of Parliament. It marks the end of conflicts and wars. All this is well known and understood. If this role were to be seriously challenged – if, for example, the monarch wanted to become a member of another denomination or faith – or if the Church were to refuse its traditional role on civic or royal occasions, the complete withdrawal of religion from the public sphere and national life would surely follow.

During the course of the last century the Church learnt to practise its historic role more and more either on behalf of or, more likely, together with all the Christian denominations in this country. It is inconceivable now that other Churches are not represented in chaplaincies, at war memorials, on civic, national and royal occasions. Then towards the end of the last century the Church of England also learnt to work alongside those of other faiths as well. If the Church of England did not take account of other religious groups it would quickly forfeit the right to speak on behalf of faith and would be seriously, if not fatally, weakened as the national Church. In fact, other faiths seem both to recognize the role the state Church plays and also to welcome and support it.

It is sometimes claimed that there is something impertinent if not impossible about this. How can one denomination among many, one faith among many, in a country that has people of all faiths and none, pretend that it can act for all in celebrations and commemorations? No doubt if we were setting about creating a constitution and rituals to support national cohesion in the circumstances of today's plural nation, we might not start from here. But we are where we are, and just as the monarch has had to learn how to be monarch of all, so the monarch's Church has learnt to do the same.

Parochial

Finally, the Church of England is a parish-based Church. This is the form the Church takes in order to be the national Church, ministering to people in every place regardless of their own religious or non-religious loyalties. In the previous chapters I have written at length about what that means in the contemporary context. In each place the Church of England is in a position to meet certain needs – at times of community celebration, remembering and mourning. What is less under-stood, especially by those Anglicans who want to harden the boundaries between regular churchgoers and others, is the way the Church acts as a protector of the nation's spiritual instincts and religious sensibilities. It keeps before the English people the big questions about human existence, its meaning and its worth.

If, however, the Church were to abandon this model – the parish model – for that of the gathered Church, it would cease to be the Church of the English people and become one more Protestant denomination along the high street, competing with other churches that were also gathered congregations of the like-minded. That would be a loss of historic proportions.

One final point. A Church that is Protestant, inclusive, national and parish-based in the ways I have described above is also a Church that prepares Christians very well to take their place in a modern democracy. It provides a training for living in a plural community where citizens must learn how to live with others who do not share some or all of their opinions. At its best, it teaches more than tolerance. It teaches Anglicans to rejoice in the richness and variety of a plural world and to seek out what is of value in the traditions of others.

Lost Church?

When we put all this together we find something very curious. The Church of England – Protestant, inclusive, national, parish-based – is beginning to be rejected not so much by the people of England but by a growing number in the Church itself. This is often in the mistaken view that religion in general and Christianity and the Church of England in particular are no longer valued. Yet as I have sought to show, throughout 2011–12 there were distinct signs in the media that journalists and commentators were becoming tired of the relentless attack on religion and more willing to give faith a hearing. A YouGov poll in February 2012 was also revealing in that while it found that most people were not especially religious, 56 per cent believed that Britain was a Christian country and 61 per cent thought that it should be. In a plural society and a culture that is less friendly towards Christianity, this ought to give a great deal of encouragement. All is not as lost as we might think and the Lost Church may yet be recovered. How ironical if the place of religion in public life in this country were to be undermined not by aggressive atheists, whose ferocious attacks in the 1990s and early 2000s have passed their high-water mark, but by a certain type of Christian. The real enemies of the Church of England may not be without but within. But while some of those who are trying to change fundamentally the nature of the Church of England know exactly what they are doing, there are many more who have not understood just what is at stake. If the Church is to rediscover its mission – in the broadest sense – and find fresh courage in the coming decades, its clergy and laity will need to recover a workable theology of what it is to be the Church and, more specifically, the Church of England in contemporary, plural society. Let me turn in this final section to exploring that theme.

A theology of the Church for the Church of England

There are many ways of thinking about the Church and its mission. The theologian Paul Minear found 96 images used in the New Testament alone.[4] It is unlikely, therefore, that any one way will do justice to the reality of what the Church is and is for. In a survey of modern approaches, Avery Dulles speaks about five principal ways in which the Church has been conceived.[5] He calls them 'models': institutional, mystical communion, sacrament, herald, servant. Thus, to take just two of the models, the Roman Catholic Church would be an example of the 'institutional', while a Pentecostal church would be an instance of the 'herald'. For the former, the visible society, ordered and structured, with distinctive buildings and personnel, would be very important. For the latter, the central concern would be congregations of people committed to preach the gospel and make converts; they would be less concerned with elaborate structure or church buildings or people in clerical dress. One or other of these models has influenced the thinking and practice of particular churches down the centuries and continues to do so even when people are not conscious of the type of ecclesiology that is implicit in what they say and do. No Church is an ideal type in the sense that it fits perfectly one model; all combine different features, though each will tend to have a particular model more to the fore of its thinking than others. In the case of the Roman Catholic Church, it is an institutional Church, but it is also a Church that sees itself as in some sense a 'sacrament' – in the way that the Eucharist is a tangible and visible sign of something hidden and spiritual. Let me set out here something of the theology that has undergirded everything written in these pages about the Church of England.

In an earlier book I suggested that the role of the Church is to make God possible – to make it possible for people to find God in their lives in the contemporary age.[6] In this sense the Church continues the mission of Jesus. Those who encountered Jesus found in his words, his actions, his living and dying, the living God. This understanding of the Church's mission has sometimes been called 'incarnational'. A Church that understands its role as 'incarnational' is one that in important respects sees its mission and ministry as an extension through time of the mission and ministry of Jesus Christ. That is an idea that fits very well with the Church of England's historic understanding and practice. Let me draw out three aspects of this understanding of the role of the Church – though they will tend to overlap.

Finding the divine in the human

First, in Jesus the divine and the human meet. Those who came across Jesus in the days of his flesh were able to encounter in him and through him the unseen God. It is as if two spotlights come together on the stage to illuminate the same place. Not surprisingly, it was an experience that could be by turns unsettling, challenging, liberating, threatening or bewildering. 'Who is this that even the winds and waves obey him?', the disciples murmured in the boat. 'Who gave you power to forgive sins?', the Pharisees wanted to know. 'He speaks with authority and not as the scribes', the people said. As the Church reflected on the totality of this experience in the light of the resurrection, it led Christians to speak of Jesus as the 'image of the invisible

God', the one in whom 'all the fullness of God was pleased to dwell', the Word made flesh, Emmanuel, God with us (Colossians 1.15, 19; cf. John 1). This is the Christian claim that most sharply distinguishes Christianity from the other monotheistic faiths, Judaism and Islam. If it is not true, then it is, as they would insist, the most appalling act of idolatry and blasphemy – confusing the created with the Creator, the material with the spiritual. If it is true, then the unknown God can be known in Jesus Christ.

A Church that sees itself as the continuation of the Incarnation down the years and across the continents is one that recognizes that it is both a divine society and a human organization. It may be all too human at times – weak, apathetic, lacklustre, sinful – and yet it is a chosen instrument of God by which and through which he will continue to reveal himself to the world, to challenge as well as to heal. An incarnational Church has a sense of the Church as part of the gospel, not simply the means of conveying the gospel.

And yet this does not mean that the Church cannot recognize the presence of God beyond its own boundaries. Jesus acknowledged others who were close to God, those who were 'not far from the kingdom of heaven', and found faith in people in ways that would have raised eyebrows in his day – in a Roman centurion, in a woman, in prostitutes and sinners who were entering the kingdom of God before scribes and Pharisees, in a condemned and dying thief. The Church of Jesus Christ trains itself to do the same.

Recognizing the Church as both a human institution as well as a divine society also means that Anglicans do not have to pretend that the Church is a perfect organization. Faults can be acknowledged and do not have to be explained away or covered up or 'spun'.

Not everyone was able to glimpse God in Christ. Yet for those who did, their lives could be transformed. So with the Church.

Purposive presence

This brings us to the second feature of the incarnational Church. It is present in a place for a purpose, and that purpose is not only to make better the lives of individuals but through them to enable local communities to flourish as well – because it is only when a community flourishes that the individuals who live there can live well. 'Seek the welfare of the city,' God told the exiled Jews through the mouth of the prophet Jeremiah, '. . . for in its welfare you will find your welfare' (Jeremiah 29.7). This is why the Church of England is parochially organized. It is a means of being committed to a place and the people of that place, for a purpose. There are Christian denominations that make much of the spectacular transformation of human lives through the power of the Holy Spirit – the rally at which a paralysed woman gets out of her wheelchair and walks, the miracles of healing associated with a shrine, the career criminal whose life is turned around following his conversion. But these spectacular changes are often performed away from the living or working context of those who are healed or changed. Anglicans are glad to see all these transformations, yet less persuaded by them than more mundane changes that they would see as equally miraculous, though miracles with long histories and where change is sometimes a matter of two paces forward and one back. For all its weaknesses and foolishness, the Church of England still produces many fine Christians who quietly go about the business of being Christians in their workplaces and communities, transforming them by their patience, kindness and generosity – their quiet presence, often over long periods of time. An incarnational Church is a modest Church even while it acknowledges that it is for many the place where God is known.

This is why many church plants in the end fail. They are not genuinely rooted in a community, and the leaders are like impatient gardeners who want instant results. But these are seeds that spring up vigorously at first only to wither away.

Modesty, humility, service

The third aspect of the incarnational Church is its recognition that it must not take for granted its presence in the life of the community and the nation. It is where it is as a result of service not privilege. For obvious historic reasons, the Church of England does occupy a privileged place in English society. At a national level, its Supreme Governor is the monarch, its bishops sit in Parliament and many state occasions include Anglican acts of worship. At the local level there is still an expectation that Anglican clergy take a lead or are prominently involved in whatever rites and ceremonies are needed to bring communities together on particular occasions. Yet a modest Church, a Church that knows that God works through others, whether people of faith or not, can adapt to a changing and more plural society in ways that enable a wider participation and sharing, but also keep alive an acknowledgement of God.

This understanding of the Church makes sense of both the concept of the parish and of the parish priest. Because the parish churches have seen themselves in this way, their clergy have developed a particular kind of relationship with people in the community and this has enabled them to have a role in the community – and in national life – that is not necessarily granted to the clergy of churches that have a different model to guide them. Anglican clergy are greeted in the street as 'Vicar' or 'Padre'. They are recognized as the visible representatives of both the local church and the wider Church in the world. It is understood that they are on the side of those who greet them and will work for their well-being and that of their community. This recognition has been hard won over many centuries of commitment to the parish, its people and their welfare, material as well as spiritual. There is an old Jewish joke that bears witness to this widespread and enduring sense about the availability of the Anglican clergy and to the idea of belonging that I am proposing. It has often been affectionately told to me by Jewish friends. An elderly Jew, living in a remote village, is very ill and close to death. The rabbi lives a good distance away and there is a ferocious storm outside. The dying man instructs his wife to send for the vicar. She remonstrates with him. 'You have been a pious Jew all your life and you want me to send for the vicar?' 'I know', he says, 'I would send for the rabbi but the weather is terrible.'

That understanding of the vicar could be quickly lost, and once lost unlikely to be recovered in any foreseeable future. So there is a great deal at stake in the rather dangerous experiment that some dioceses – such as the one whose vision statement I highlighted above – are now permitting to happen.

Church plants are generally incompatible with the incarnational model of the Church by which the Church of England has been guided in the past – unless they are a group that the parish church has itself planted in its own geographical parish for some particular reason. If there is, for example, a housing estate at a distance from the parish church, it might make sense to establish a eucharistic congregation in a local school. But churches that 'plant' in another parish are implicitly taking as their model something that is quite alien to the Church of England. It is alien and also destructive, undermining the incarnational mission of the Church of England to the people and parishes of the nation.

Conclusion

My aim in writing this book has been twofold. First, I wanted to remind contemporary members of the Church of England of the many millions of our fellow citizens who still 'belong' to the Church even if they are not regular attenders and their faith is not as orthodox or coherent as we might like. Despite several decades of assault on faith in general and Christianity in particular, many still value the Church of England's commitment to both national life and local communities. But in the second place, I wanted to alert Anglicans to the fact that this understanding of the Church is being increasingly threatened not by the enemies of Christianity, but by fellow Christians who have little time for those whose faith is not expressed in terms of commitment to a prescribed set of beliefs or regular attendance. In the past, the existence within the Church of England of those who took this view was not a cause for concern. They were a minority, they observed the discipline of the parish boundary and they were influenced by the theology, implicit and explicit, of the Book of Common Prayer. But this is no longer the case. The loss of the Prayer Book, the movement for 'fresh expressions', the compulsion to 'plant' new congregations, the rejection of the incarnational model and the disregard of the parish system is threatening the traditional role of the Church of England. That is the Lost Church in the title of the book. It is that Church that we must find again.

Notes

-------◆◆◆-------

Introduction

1 Grace Davie, *Religion in Britain since 1945: Believing without belonging* (Oxford: Blackwell, 1994).
2 The 2001 Census was the first to ask about people's religious identity. The results were: Christian 72 per cent; Muslim 3 per cent; Hindu 1 per cent; Sikh 0.6 per cent; Jewish 0.5 per cent; Buddhist 0.3 per cent; any other religion 0.3 per cent; no religion 15 per cent; no response 8 per cent.

1 Belonging

1 The British Social Attitudes Survey is published annually by the National Centre for Social Research. The figures here are from the twenty-sixth report of 2010 as updated in 2011.
2 Paul Heelas and Linda Woodhead, *The Spiritual Revolution: Why religion is giving way to spirituality* (Oxford: Blackwell, 2004).
3 A YouGov poll found something similar in 2012: <www.labs.yougov.co.uk/news/2012/02/17/britain-christian-country>.
4 This understanding of the Church of England's vocation is examined in Wesley Carr, *Say One for Me: The Church of England in the next decade* (London: SPCK, 1992).
5 From an interview by Luke Coppen, 'Thinking space', *The Spectator*, 17/24 December 2011.
6 Interview on BBC TV *News*, 7 April 2012. It is possible that the presenting clergy did not make this clear to the Archbishop.
7 It was this incident that I had in mind when writing about infant baptism in *Secular Lives, Sacred Hearts: The role of the Church in a time of no religion* (London: SPCK, 2004), p. 56.
8 <www.yourchurchwedding.org>.
9 See the report by the University of Hull at <www.2.hull.ac.uk/fass/pdf/final.pdf>.

10 *Sunday Telegraph*, 26 October 2010.

11 Simon Jenkins, 'At this time of year we must thank God for churches', *The Guardian*, 23 December 2011.

12 Alain de Botton, *Religion for Atheists: A non-believer's guide to the uses of religion* (London: Hamish Hamilton, 2012), pp. 43–50.

13 *The Times*, 4 February 2012.

14 Mary Warnock, *Dishonest to God: On keeping religion out of politics* (London and New York: Continuum, 2010), pp. 160–1.

15 Bernice Martin, 'Church and culture' in Wesley Carr (ed.), *Say One for Me: The Church of England in the next decade* (London: SPCK, 1992), p. 101.

2 Attending

1 Brierley Consultancy, *21 Concerns for 21st Century Christians* (Tonbridge: ADBC Publishers, 2011). Web: <www.brierleyconsultancy.com>.

2 Trevor Cooper and Sarah Brown (eds), *Pews, Benches and Chairs: Church seating in English parish churches from the fourteenth century to the present* (London: The Ecclesiology Society, 2011).

3 Brierley Consultancy, *21 Concerns*.

4 Brierley Consultancy, *21 Concerns*.

5 Paul Heelas and Linda Woodhead, *The Spiritual Revolution: Why religion is giving way to spirituality* (Oxford: Blackwell, 2004).

6 Brierley Consultancy, *21 Concerns*.

7 Callum G. Brown, *The Death of Christian Britain: Understanding secularisation 1800–2000* (London and New York: Routledge, 2001).

8 Brown, *Death of Christian Britain*, p. 88.

9 Brown, *Death of Christian Britain*, p. 58.

10 Coventry Patmore, *Angel in the House* (Milton Keynes: Dodo Press, undated). The poem was published in two parts in 1854 and 1856.

11 Woolf said this in a speech to a branch of the National Society for Women's Service, 21 January 1931. It was published posthumously in *The Death of the Moth and Other Essays* (1942). Virginia Woolf, *Killing the Angel in the House: Seven essays* (London: Penguin, 1995), p. 3.

12 Families and Households 2001–2011, Office for National Statistics, January 2012.

13 *Church Times*, 13 April 2012.

14 Brierley Consultancy, *21 Concerns*.

15 <www.pewresearch.org>.

16 *The Tablet*, 17/24 December 2011.

17 Bob Holman writing in *The Observer*, 26 February 2012.

18 Jeanette Winterson, *Oranges Are Not the Only Fruit* (London: Vintage, 2001), p. 53.

19 Roger Scruton, *England: An elegy* (London and New York: Continuum, 2006), p. 106.

20 Giles Coren, 'Why I'm pro antidisestablishmentarianism', *The Times*, 8 February 2012.

21 Tim Lott, 'Father, I have sinned – I'm an atheist', *The Times*, 13 December 2010.

22 Alain de Botton, 'An atheist at Christmas: Oh come all ye faithless', *The Guardian*, 24 December 2011. See also Alain de Botton, *Religion for Atheists: A non-believer's guide to the uses of religion* (London: Hamish Hamilton 2012).

23 Daniel Finkelstein, 'It's easy to mock religion, but then what?', *The Times* 15 February 2012.

24 Janice Turner, 'God may not be great, but religion can be', *The Times*, 28 January 2012.

25 Turner, 'God may not be great'.

26 Turner, 'God may not be great'.

27 John Gray, 'Religion for atheists is a nice idea, but hardly new', *The Guardian*, 3 March 2012.

28 Philip Larkin, *Collected Poems* (London: Marvell Press, 1988), pp. 97–8.

29 Richard Holloway, *Leaving Alexandria: A memoir of faith and doubt* (Edinburgh: Canongate Books, 2012), p. 253.

3 Believing

1 Keith Robbins, *History, Religion and Identity in Modern Britain* (London: Hambledon, 1993), p. 95.

2 Frank Prochaska, *Christianity and Social Service in Modern Britain: The disinherited Spirit* (New York and Oxford: Oxford University Press, 2006).

3 RDFRS UK, Press Release 1, 14 February 2012.

4 Richard Holloway, *Leaving Alexandria: A memoir of faith and doubt* (Edinburgh: Canongate Books, 2012), chapter 6, 'Angel of the Gorbals'.

5 Holloway, *Leaving Alexandria*, pp. 121–2.

6 A. R. Vidler (ed.), *Soundings: Essays concerning Christian understanding* (Cambridge: Cambridge University Press, 1962).

7 John Habgood, 'The uneasy truce between science and religion' in Vidler (ed.), *Soundings*, pp. 23–41.

8 John A. T. Robinson, *Honest to God* (London: SCM Press, 1963). See also John A. T. Robinson and David Edwards, *The Honest to God Debate* (London: SCM Press, 1963).

9 Dietrich Bonhoeffer, *Letters and Papers from Prison* (London: SCM Press, 1953).

10 Mark Chapman, 'Theology in the public arena: the case of South Bank religion' in Jane Garnett, Matthew Grimley, Alana Harris, William Whyte, Sarah Williams (eds), *Re-defining Christian Britain: Post 1945 perspectives* (London: SCM Press, 2007), pp. 92–4.

11 Church of England, Commission on Urban Priority Areas: *Faith in the City: A call for action by Church and Nation* (London: Church House Publishing, 1985).

12 Alan Billings, *Making God Possible. The task of ordained ministry present and future* (London: SPCK, 2010), pp. 123–9.

13 Charles Taylor, *A Secular Age* (Cambridge, MA and London: Belknap Press, 2007), p. 473.

14 *Hamlet*, Act 1, scene 3.

15 From the Second Theological Oration, sections IV and V.

16 Exodus 20.4. The warning is repeated throughout the Old Testament: e.g. Leviticus 19.4 and Deuteronomy 4.15–19.

17 Andrew Motion, 'I've seen the light. And it flickers on and off', *The Times*, 18 December 2010.

18 In an interview on BBC TV *News*.

19 Richard Williams, 'In times of trouble, the urge to appeal to a higher power remains', *The Guardian*, 27 March 2012.

20 <www.labs.yougov.co.uk/news/2012/02/17/britain-christiancountry/>.

21 This is a theme in John Cottingham, *Why Believe?* (London: Continuum, 2009).

22 Brian Mountford, *Christian Atheist: Belonging without believing* (Winchester and Washington, DC: O-Books, 2010), p. 47.

4 Reclaiming Lost Church

1 Peter Brierley, cited in 'Hot and bothered: The rise of evangelicalism is shaking up the established church', *The Economist*, 10 March 2012.

2 *The Guardian*, 23 March 2012.

3 John Calvin, *Calvin's Ecclesiastical Advice*, trans. Mary Beaty and Benjamin W. Farley (Edinburgh: T & T Clark, 1991), pp. 139ff.

4 Paul Minear, *Images of the Church in the New Testament* (London: James Clarke, 2007).

5 Avery Dulles, *Models of the Church* (New York: Image Books, 1978).

6 Alan Billings, *Making God Possible: The task of ordained ministry present and future* (London: SPCK, 2010).

Bibliography

Archbishop of Canterbury's Commission on Urban Priority Areas, *Faith in the City: A call for action by Church and Nation* (London: Church House Publishing, 1985).

Archbishops' Commission on Rural Areas, *Faith in the Countryside* (Worthing: Churchman Publishing, 1990).

Armstrong, Karen, *The Case for God: What religion really means* (London: Bodley Head, 2009).

Berger, Peter, *The Sacred Canopy: Elements of a sociological theory of religion* (Garden City NY: Anchor Books, 1969).

Billings, Alan, *Secular Lives, Sacred Hearts: The role of the Church in a time of no religion* (London: SPCK, 2004).

Billings, Alan, *Making God Possible: The task of ordained ministry present and future* (London: SPCK, 2010).

Bonhoeffer, Dietrich, *Letters and Papers from Prison* (London: SCM Press, 1953).

Bradley, Ian, *Abide with Me: The world of Victorian hymns* (London: SCM Press, 1997).

Brierley, Peter, *The Tide is Running Out* (London: Christian Research, 2000).

Brown, Callum G., *The Death of Christian Britain: Understanding secularisation 1800–2000* (London and New York: Routledge, 2001).

Bruce, Steve, *Religion in the Modern World* (Oxford: Oxford University Press, 1996).

Bruce, Steve, *God is Dead: Secularization in the West* (Oxford: Blackwell, 2002).

Calvin, John, *Calvin's Ecclesiastical Advice*, trans. Mary Beaty and Benjamin W. Farley (Edinburgh: T & T Clark, 1991).

Carr, Wesley, *Brief Encounters: Pastoral ministry through the occasional offices* (London: SPCK, 1985).

Carr, Wesley, *Say One For Me: The Church of England in the next decade* (London: SPCK, 1992).

Cocksworth, Christopher and Brown, Rosalind, *Exploring Priestly Identity* (Norwich: Canterbury Press, 2002).

Croft, Steven (ed.), *Mission-Shaped Questions* (London: Church House Publishing, 2008).

Croft, Steven and Mobsby, Ian (eds), *Ancient Faith, Future Mission: Fresh expressions in the sacramental tradition* (Norwich: Canterbury Press, 2009).

Davie, Grace, *Religion in Britain since 1945: Believing without belonging* (Oxford: Blackwell, 1994).

Davie, Grace, *Religion in Modern Europe: A memory mutates* (Oxford: Oxford University Press, 2000).

Davison, Andrew and Milbank, Alison, *For the Parish: A critique of fresh expressions* (London: SCM Press, 2010).

de Botton, Alain, *Religion for Atheists. A non-believer's guide to the uses of religion* (London: Hamish Hamilton, 2012).

Dulles, Avery, *Models of the Church* (New York: Image Books, 1978).

Eagleton, Terry, *Reason, Faith, and Revolution: Reflections on the God debate* (New Haven, NY: Yale University Press, 2009).

Furedi, Frank, *Therapy Culture: Cultivating vulnerability in an anxious age* (London: Routledge, 2004).

Garnett, Jane, Grimley, Matthew, Harris, Alana, Whyte, William and Williams, Sarah (eds), *Re-defining Christian Britain: Post 1945 perspectives* (London: SCM Press, 2007).

Heelas, Paul and Woodhead, Linda, *The Spiritual Revolution: Why religion is giving way to spirituality* (Oxford: Blackwell, 2004).

Hervieu-Leger, Daniele, *Religion as a Chain of Memory*, trans. Simon Lee (New Brunswick, NJ: Rutgers University Press, 2000).

Holloway, Richard, *Leaving Alexandria: A memoir of faith and doubt* (Edinburgh: Canongate Books, 2012).

Hull, John M., *Mission-shaped Church: A theological response* (London: SCM Press, 2006).

Jenkins, Timothy, *Religion in English Everyday Life: An ethnographic approach* (New York and Oxford: Berghahn Books, 1999).

Lewis-Anthony, Justin, *If You Meet George Herbert on the Road, Kill Him: Radically re-thinking priestly ministry* (London: Mowbray, 2009).

Lindbeck, George, *The Nature of Doctrine: Religion and theology in a postliberal age* (Philadelphia: Westminster Press, 1984).

McLeod, Hugh, *The Religious Crisis of the 1960s* (Oxford: Oxford University Press, 2007).

Martin, David, *The Future of Christianity: Reflections on violence and democracy, religion and secularization* (London: Ashgate, 2011).

Minear, Paul, *Images of the Church in the New Testament* (London: James Clark, 2007).

Mountford, Brian, *Christian Atheist: Belonging without believing* (Winchester and Washington, DC: O-Books, 2010).

Nelstrop, Louise and Percy, Martyn (eds), *Evaluating Fresh Expressions: Explorations in emerging church* (Norwich: Canterbury Press, 2008).

Niebuhr, H. Richard, *Christ and Culture* (New York: HarperCollins, 2007).

Pritchard, John, *The Life and Work of a Priest* (London: SPCK, 2007).

Prochaska, Frank, *Christianity and Social Service in Modern Britain: The disinherited Spirit* (New York and Oxford: Oxford University Press, 2006).

Radcliffe, Timothy, *Why Go to Church?* (London: Continuum, 2008).

Ramsey, Michael, *The Christian Priest Today* (London: SPCK, 1985).

Redfern, Alastair, *Ministry and Priesthood* (London: Darton, Longman & Todd, 1999).

Robbins, Keith, *History, Religion and Identity in Modern Britain* (London: Hambledon, 1993).

Robinson, John A. T., *Honest to God* (London: SCM Press, 1963).

Robinson, John A. T. and Edwards, David, *The Honest to God Debate* (London: SCM Press, 1963).

Russell, Anthony, *The Country Parson* (London: SPCK, 1993).

Scruton, Roger, *England: An elegy* (London and New York: Continuum, 2006).

Smith, Alan and Hopkinson, Jill (eds), *Faith and the Future of the Countryside: Pastoral and theological perspectives on rural sustainability* (Norwich: Canterbury Press, 2012).

Taylor, Charles, *A Secular Age* (Cambridge, MA and London: Belknap Press, 1997).

Vidler, Alec (ed.), *Soundings: Essays concerning Christian understanding* (Cambridge: Cambridge University Press, 1962).

Warnock, Mary, *Dishonest to God: On keeping religion out of politics* (London and New York: Continuum, 2010).

Winterson, Jeanette, *Oranges Are Not the Only Fruit* (London: Vintage, 2001).

Whittle, Peter, *Look At Me: Celebrating the self in modern Britain* (London: The Social Affairs Unit, 2008).

Woolf, Virginia, *Killing the Angel in the House: Seven essays* (London: Penguin, 1995).

Wright, Frank, *The Pastoral Nature of the Ministry* (London: SPCK, 1980).

Index